Muhammad Ali

HEAVYWEIGHT CHAMPION

Black Americans of Achievement

LEGACY EDITION

Muhammad Ali

Frederick Douglass

W.E.B. Du Bois

Marcus Garvey

Alex Haley

Langston Hughes

Jesse Jackson

Coretta Scott King

Martin Luther King, Jr.

Malcolm X

Thurgood Marshall

Jesse Owens

Rosa Parks

Colin Powell

Sojourner Truth

Harriet Tubman

Nat Turner

Booker T. Washington

Black Americans of Achievement

LEGACY EDITION

Muhammad Ali

HEAVYWEIGHT CHAMPION

Jack Rummel

With additional text written by
Gloria Blakely

Consulting Editor, Revised Edition
Heather Lehr Wagner

Senior Consulting Editor, First Edition
Nathan Irvin Huggins
Director, W.E.B. Du Bois Institute
for Afro-American Research
Harvard University

CHELSEA HOUSE
PUBLISHERS
A Haights Cross Communications Company
Philadelphia

COVER: Boxing legend Muhammad Ali poses for a photo after a 1999 interview in New York.

CHELSEA HOUSE PUBLISHERS

VP, NEW PRODUCT DEVELOPMENT Sally Cheney
DIRECTOR OF PRODUCTION Kim Shinners
CREATIVE MANAGER Takeshi Takahashi
MANUFACTURING MANAGER Diann Grasse

Staff for MUHAMMAD ALI

EXECUTIVE EDITOR Lee Marcott
ASSISTANT EDITOR Alexis Browsh
PRODUCTION EDITOR Noelle Nardone
PHOTO EDITOR Sarah Bloom
SERIES AND COVER DESIGNER Keith Trego
LAYOUT 21st Century Publishing and Communications, Inc.

A Haights Cross Communications Company

www.chelseahouse.com

First Printing

9 8 7 6 5 4 3 2 1

Library of Congress Cataloging-in-Publication Data

Rummel, Jack.
   Muhammad Ali /Jack Rummel; with additional text by Gloria Blakely.
      p. cm.—(Black Americans of achievement)
Includes bibliographical references and index.
   ISBN 0-7910-8156-7 (hardcover) — ISBN 0-7910-8330-6 (pbk.)
   1. Ali, Muhammad, 1942– —Juvenile literature. 2. Boxers (Sports)—United States—
Biography—Juvenile literature. I. Blakely, Gloria. II. Title. III. Series.
GV1132.A44R86 2004
796.83'092—dc22

                                                                                    2004015304

Contents

Introduction

Nearly 20 years ago, Chelsea House Publishers began to publish the first volumes in the series called BLACK AMERICANS OF ACHIEVEMENT. This series eventually numbered over a hundred books and profiled outstanding African Americans from many walks of life. Today, if you ask school teachers and school librarians what comes to mind when you mention Chelsea House, many will say—"Black Americans of Achievement."

The mix of individuals whose lives we covered was eclectic, to say the least. Some were well known—Muhammad Ali and Dr. Martin Luther King, Jr, for example. But others, such as Harriet Tubman and Sojourner Truth, were lesser-known figures who were introduced to modern readers through these books. The individuals profiled were chosen for their actions, their deeds, and ultimately their influence on the lives of others and their impact on our nation as a whole. By sharing these stories of unique Americans, we hoped to illustrate how ordinary individuals can be transformed by extraordinary circumstances to become people of greatness. We also hoped that these special stories would encourage young-adult readers to make their own contribution to a better world. Judging from the many wonderful letters we have received about the BLACK AMERICANS OF ACHIEVEMENT biographies over the years from students, librarians, and teachers, they have certainly fulfilled the goal of inspiring others!

Now, some 20 years later, we are publishing 18 volumes of the original BLACK AMERICANS OF ACHIEVEMENT series in revised editions to bring the books into the twenty-first century and make them available to a new generation of young-adult readers. The selection was based on the importance of these figures to American life and the popularity of the original books with our readers. These revised editions have a new full-color design and, wherever possible, we have added color photographs. The books have new features, including quotes from the writings and speeches of leaders and interesting and unusual facts about their lives. The concluding section of each book gives new emphasis to the legacy of these men and women for the current generation of readers.

The lives of these African-American leaders are unique and remarkable. By transcending the barriers that racism placed in their paths, they are examples of the power and resiliency of the human spirit and are an inspiration to readers.

We present these wonderful books to our audience for their reading pleasure.

Lee M. Marcott

Chelsea House Publishers

August 2004

Miss Velvet Green

On a warm and humid day on April 28, 1967, Muhammad Ali, the heavyweight boxing champion of the world, does not go to the gym for a workout. Instead, the 25-year-old fighter makes his way to the federal courthouse in Houston, Texas. Ali, whose legal residence is the state of Kentucky rather than Texas, has nonetheless come to know Houston quite well: Only two months earlier, he fought and won a brutal 15-round match against Ernie Terrell in Houston's Astrodome; and three months before that, in November 1966, he fought Cleveland Williams in an easier match at that same venue. Ali is not in Houston on this spring day to fight any one man, however. He has been summoned to Texas to report for induction into the armed forces of the United States of America.

A large crowd of onlookers has gathered at the courthouse by the time Ali and his lawyers arrive. A mob of reporters and photographers rush him as he gets out of a taxi at the foot of

Despite facing a possible prison sentence, loss of his title, and ban from boxing, heavyweight champion Muhammad Ali refused to be inducted into the Army because of his religious convictions. Here, Ali is escorted from a Houston courthouse on April 28, 1967.

the courthouse steps. These spectators have not come to wish him well at the beginning of a stint in the army. Instead, they are there either to support or vilify him as he is about to tell U.S. Selective Service Board officials that he is not destined to become just another GI. He has already promised in public to refuse induction into the army, thus risking a long jail sentence and the possible ruin of his professional career.

Ali is bombarded with questions as he and his entourage— his bodyguards and aides—mount the courthouse steps. A group of black students from Texas Southern University march back and forth across the street. From behind police barricades, they shout their support for Ali and hold up signs that demand, "Stay Home, Muhammad Ali." A group of hippies also yell support for him. Other bystanders are not so sympathetic.

At the top of the courthouse steps, Ali is joined by one of his trainers, Drew "Bundini" Brown. While the crowd of reporters jostle around them, Brown, who is known simply as Bundini, gestures across the street. "There she is now," he says.

Ali's gaze searches the crowd until he finds her. He has seen her before; she has been haunting him on his recent trips to Houston. She is a stylish white woman, perhaps 40 years old. With her is a chauffeur and another man. As before, she is wearing a dress of green velvet.

A WORLD OF DISAPPROVAL

Ali's most vivid memory of this woman is from after his tough and bloody fight with Terrell. That night, as he made his way through the crowd after the fight, she appeared before him with pen and paper and asked for his autograph. Ali clearly remembered her face from after his recent fight with Williams. "I come to all your fights," the woman he has since named Miss Velvet Green said to him. "I will keep coming," she continued as she neatly folded the paper containing the autograph he had given her, "until I see them take you out on a stretcher. God won't always let evil win."

IN HIS OWN WORDS...

Ali testified in his previous Selective Service hearing:

> ... and so, I wouldn't turn down so many millions and jeopardize my life walking the streets of the South and all of America with no bodyguards if I wasn't sincere in every bit of what the Holy Qur'an and the teachings of the Honorable Elijah Muhammad tell us.

For Ali, this nameless woman in the green velvet dress has come to personify the hatred directed toward him because of his exuberant style, personal beliefs, and religious convictions. For every man or woman cheering for him to win in or out of the ring, there is a Miss Velvet Green hoping to see him knocked out, sent to prison, or even killed. These intense feelings have been aroused because Ali is more than just another heavyweight champion. For some, he is a symbol of black pride; for others, he is an example of the kind of courage one must have if one is to protest against an unpopular war; and for many more—including Miss Velvet Green—he is the incarnation of threatening and unwanted social change.

She stands on the other side of the street, waiting until Ali spots her. Then, assured that she has been noticed by him, she begins to leave. Her figure in green is the last thing that Ali sees before he turns around to confront the power of the U.S. government.

Cassius Clay of Louisville

Muhammad Ali was born into a working-class household in Louisville, Kentucky, on January 18, 1942. He was originally named Cassius Marcellus Clay, Jr., after both his father and a prominent nineteenth-century abolitionist and politician. He legally changed his name to Muhammad Ali from Cassius Clay when he was 21 years old.

The eldest of two sons, Cassius was part of a closely knit and loving family. His mother, Odessa Grady Clay, was affectionately called "Bird" by her family. She worked as a cook and housecleaner. His father, Cassius, Sr., was known as Cash. He worked as a sign painter to support his family. He also painted murals on the walls of black churches around Louisville to earn additional money and to exercise his artistic talent.

By all accounts, Cash Clay was a warm-hearted man. He had a bit of an actor in him, and he loved to sing. In the family's home at night, he would imitate his favorite crooners:

Nat "King" Cole, Bing Crosby, and Russ Colombo. His love for the entertainment world eventually prompted him to name his second son Rudolph Valentino Clay after the popular silent film star.

Watching his father at work and at play, young Cassius sensed that despite his apparent gaiety, his father felt frustrated. He was someone with the ability to be more than just a sign painter. In another city or at another time, he might have been able to become a successful artist. Opportunities for blacks were limited in Louisville, though, and he was only offered the chance to paint on church walls, on the sides of buildings, and on large billboards.

The future heavyweight champion made a vow early on to leave the South. He wanted more out of life than a place such as Louisville could give him.

While black workers in Kentucky were not very well paid, the Clays were neither the poorest nor the wealthiest of black families in Louisville. They never went hungry, yet there was seldom any money left over for items that many American families took for granted. Hamburgers and hot dogs were standard fare at the dinner table; chicken and potatoes were considered extravagances. The family's clothes were always secondhand. The four-room house in which they lived was in constant need of repair. The roof leaked and the porch was in danger of falling down, but the money that Cassius's parents earned went for essential items first: food, clothing, bills, a used car, and gasoline. After paying for these basic needs, they usually did not have any money left.

Cassius and his brother, Rudy, did own bicycles, but even these were necessities. Their parents did not have enough money for the two boys to take a bus to school, so they rode their bikes instead.

The Clays lived in Louisville's West End section, which was one of the city's three black ghettos. When Cassius was growing up, there were laws in many states that were aimed specifically at keeping blacks and whites separated. Known as Jim Crow laws, they forbade blacks such as Cassius from going into certain stores to buy groceries or refreshments or into certain theaters to see a movie. These laws also established many separate facilities for blacks and whites, including schools and hotels. In downtown Louisville, blacks were allowed to shop in department stores but were not allowed to eat in the store cafeterias. Nor were they allowed to eat in many of the cafes or restaurants in the city's main commercial area. Not surprisingly, such restrictions caused feelings of resentment among many blacks.

Cassius's childhood was filled with incidents in which he was denied entrance to a place where whites were allowed to go. By the time he was a teenager attending DuValle Junior High School, he felt compelled to react against the pressure of being a black in a predominantly white society. His actions were touched off by a story that he heard in 1955 about the murder of a 14 year old from Chicago named Emmett Till.

While Till was visiting his uncle in Mississippi during a summer vacation, he was beaten until unrecognizable, shot, and thrown into a river by three white men who may have been members of the white supremacist organization known as the Ku Klux Klan. They had abducted Till because his appearance matched the description of a young black who had "spoken to" a white woman. (The men claimed that Till had made sexual advances to the woman.) Yet they denied killing him—even though a number of witnesses offered damning evidence against them. The men were tried by an all-white jury in Mississippi and were found not guilty of Till's murder; a grand jury also refused to indict them on the charge of kidnapping. The freed men later confessed their crimes to Bradford Huie for the price of four thousand dollars. (For additional information on the murder of Emmett Till and the reaction to his death in the community, enter "Emmett Till" into any search engine and browse the sites listed.)

The purpose of such lynchings was to frighten blacks throughout America into remaining in a position of economic and social subservience. Till's mother fought this vicious strategy. To confront the Klan as well as to provoke outrage against the kind of men who would murder an unarmed and innocent boy, she displayed her son's mutilated body as it lay at rest in an open casket. Thousands of people—many of them total strangers to the family—came to pay their respects to the young man and to show their support for his mother and the cause of racial justice. Her actions were one of the first public expressions of outrage in what would become known as the Modern Civil Rights Movement.

The news of this atrocity was given worldwide coverage in the press. Perhaps the most graphic and detailed reports appeared in black newspapers around the country. *Jet* published a photo of the adolescent's mutilated body. Its very sight contradicted the free humanitarian image American governing officials were trying to convey internationally during the Cold War against communism. Closer to home the reality of this lynching seized the black community's attention and soon galvanized African-American churches into action. The NAACP saw Till as a young martyr who should not be forgotten. A civil rights wave stood ready to cascade from the horizon and Till's name was a rallying cry.

The story deeply affected Cassius, whose emotions ranged from shock to sadness to anger. He felt a need to strike back at white society, which he held responsible for Till's death. Not knowing what to do—although feeling the need to act, no matter in how futile or pointless a way—he sneaked out of his house one night and met up with a friend at the West End railroad station. The two boys placed some pieces of metal on some of the tracks in the hope of derailing a train.

After doing this, Cassius noticed a poster nailed to a lamp-post. The image displayed on the poster infuriated him, and he began hurling stones at the sign until it was ripped to

Even as a child, Ali was outraged at the racism and injustice he encountered in the world. After the murder of Emmett Till, he was so upset at America's hypocrisy and inability to protect blacks that he defiled a U.S. Army recruiting poster, like the one seen here.

pieces. The poster had shown a stern, elderly white man with a long, wispy white beard: "Uncle Sam," the symbol of the U.S. government. Below his visage were the words "I Want You." The poster was a recruiting advertisement for the U.S. army.

DISCOVERING A FUTURE

Cassius's actions at the train station were largely out of character; throughout his youth, he kept out of trouble and attended school regularly. Yet he and Till had been about the same age, so to Cassius there seemed no reason other than pure chance as to why Till had been killed and he had not. He was beginning to discover—as many teenagers do—that the world is a place where grave injustices can be committed.

A similar discovery took place on an afternoon in 1954, the year before Till's death. Cassius was riding on a new bicycle, accompanied by his friend Johnny Willis. His bike was a Schwinn, with red lights, chrome trim, and whitewall tires. It had been given to him for Christmas by his father.

On that day, the two boys were riding up and down the streets of Louisville with no particular purpose in mind. When it began to rain, they rode over to the Columbia Auditorium to dry off. Willis knew that a bazaar called the Louisville Home Show was being held in the auditorium and that free hot dogs, popcorn, and candy were being served there.

Cassius and his friend stayed at the auditorium for part of the afternoon. When they left the building to return home, Cassius discovered that his bicycle had been stolen. He immediately became upset; he was not looking forward to telling his father what had happened. Consequently, he rushed around the neighborhood, trying unsuccessfully to locate his bike.

Someone finally directed Cassius to a white policeman named Joe Martin, who ran a boxing program in the Columbia Auditorium gym, which was across the street from Nazareth College, where Cassius worked part-time. In the gym, Martin wrote down what the boy told him about the theft. By the end of their interview, however, Cassius had nearly forgotten his troubles. The scene inside the gym, which was filled with boxers jumping rope, shadow boxing, and popping the speed bags, mesmerized him. Martin must have noticed this, for he gave Cassius an application to join the boxing program, which ran from six to eight o'clock in the evening, Monday through Friday.

Cassius took an application form but did not make a decision about joining the program until the following Saturday. That afternoon, he happened to tune in to a local television show called "Tomorrow's Champions," which featured amateur boxing matches in Louisville. There on television, working as a manager and trainer in the corner of one of the boxers, was Joe Martin from the Columbia gym. Impressed by seeing Martin on television, Cassius pointed him out to his parents and told them that he wanted to give boxing a try. Although they were a little hesitant, they agreed to let him start training.

Joe Martin, Clay's First Boxing Coach

Joe Martin could not have imagined during the youngster's first year of training the talent Cassius Clay would wield in the future. "I guess I've taught a thousand boys to box, or at least tried to teach them. Cassius Clay, when he first began coming around, looked no better or worst than the majority." Martin added to his discussion with author Thomas Hauser for the biography, *Muhammad Ali: His Life and Times*, "If boxers were paid bonuses on their potential like ballplayers are, I don't know if he would have received one. He was just ordinary, and I doubt whether any scout would have thought much of him in his first year. About a year later, though, you could see that the little smart aleck—I mean, he's always been sassy—had a lot of potential. He stood out because, I guess, he had more determination than most boys, and he had the speed to get him someplace. He was a kid willing to make the sacrifices necessary to achieve something worthwhile in sports. I realized it was almost impossible to discourage him. He was easily the hardest worker of any kid I ever taught."

Not quite yet 13 years old, Cassius began his boxing career as a skinny 112-pound novice. His first sparring match was with an older and more experienced opponent who bounced enough punches off of Cassius's head to leave him dizzy, discouraged, and bleeding from the nose. After fighting for a few rounds, another young fighter came up to him and offered a few words of advice. "Don't box these older fellows first," he said. "Box the fellows who are new like you. Get someone to teach you how to do it."

Cassius started to learn what he could about boxing. Although he was a novice, his tremendous stamina helped him wear down his opponents. He was soon making appearances on "Tomorrow's Champions," and even though he was still an amateur fighter, he was paid four dollars for each appearance on the show. To a poor young fighter in 1955, this amount was a lot of money.

That same year, Cassius made it to the Kentucky State Golden Gloves championship tournament. In the tournament, he was beaten by a fighter from a rival gym in Louisville, the Grace Community Center gym. The fighter was a product of Fred Stoner's management. Soon after Cassius's defeat in this tournament, he started to train with Stoner as well as with Martin.

Cassius quickly developed a regular daily schedule. He went to school from eight in the morning until two in the afternoon, then worked for the Catholic sisters in the library of Nazareth College until six in the evening. After grabbing a quick bite to eat, he would train at Martin's gym until eight, then he would fine-tune his boxing skills at Stoner's until midnight. It was important for Cassius to set a strict schedule for himself. In order to become a champion boxer—which is what he was aiming to become—a fighter had to have a lot of discipline.

Although Cassius trained hard with Martin, he trained even harder with Stoner, who not only emphasized the fine points of counterpunching but also demanded that his boxers work on basic conditioning. Consequently, Cassius ran many miles every day and did sit-ups until his abdominal muscles hurt so much that he could not do any more. Then, for good measure, he played catch with a medicine ball so he could strengthen his midsection even more and jumped rope until his legs became extremely tired. As a result of this training, he began to win … 50 fights … 100 fights. Before long, he had won 161 amateur fights out of 167. Of the six fights that he lost, most took place at the beginning of his amateur career.

WHAT'S IN A NAME?

By the time Cassius entered Central High School, he was a seasoned amateur boxer as well as a student. One day, a teacher noted his name approvingly by saying, "Cassius Marcellus Clay, if only you could just follow in the footsteps of that great friend of Abraham Lincoln, that fighting Abolitionist whose name you carry.…" Until then, Cassius had never given much thought to his name, which he knew was also the name of a white Kentucky-born abolitionist who had lived in the nineteenth century.

Spurred on by his teacher's comment, Cassius discovered that the abolitionist Clay was a member of the aristocracy and a close relative of Senator Henry Clay's. Although he had inherited slaves and large holdings of land from his father, he eventually denounced the institution of slavery. He freed his slaves shortly before the Civil War and ran for Congress as a crusader against slavery. Even though he was defeated in his bid for Congress, he continued his abolitionist efforts. He founded an abolitionist newspaper, the *True American*, and in 1854, he helped found the Republican party, which under Abraham Lincoln became the party that legally ended slavery in the United States.

As the future heavyweight champion dug further into the facts about Clay's life, however, he discovered some disquieting information. Although Clay was opposed to slavery, he did not

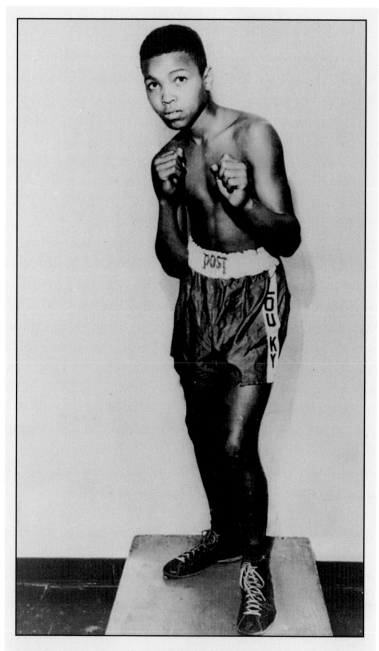

Cassius Clay became involved in boxing at age 12 and immediately showed promise. He is seen here, weighing just 85 pounds, posing before his 1954 amateur ring debut.

believe that blacks were the equals of whites. In a collection of Clay's writings, Cassius found the following:

> I am of the opinion that the Caucasian or white is the superior race; they have a larger and a better formed brain; much more developed form and exquisite structure. Modern discovery proved that the builders of pyramids and Egyptian founders of signs and letters were white....

Clay was a much more complicated and difficult person than the simple hero that Cassius was led to believe. Rather than being a true champion of racial equality, he was something of a racist. Although he had freed his slaves, he had not succeeded in freeing his mind from misguided yet popular opinion. The high school student Cassius Clay would remember this distinction. Although he said little about his discovery to his acquaintances, his given name would never sound so fine to him again.

3

Dance of the Dinosaurs

Professional boxing is divided into eight weight classes: flyweight, bantamweight, featherweight, lightweight, welterweight, middleweight, light heavyweight, and heavyweight. Fighters from the heavyweight division are the ones who have most consistently grabbed the attention of the public. Perhaps it is because they are the biggest men, the gladiators; perhaps it is because their division has produced the most colorful fighters. Whatever the reason, the heavyweight champions stand at the pinnacle of boxing, and their names have the ring of poetry to the ears of boxing fans: John L. Sullivan, "Gentleman Jim" Corbett, Jack Johnson, Gene Tunney, Jack Dempsey, Joe Louis, Rocky Marciano.

Even when Cassius Clay was a 112-pound 13-year-old flyweight, he dreamed of one day becoming the heavyweight champion. As soon as he began training as a fighter, he learned that heavyweights had a mystique about them that was all their

Boxing, and especially heavyweight boxing, has been popular in America for at least two hundred years. The huge crowd in this photograph gathered to watch an 1889 bare-knuckle bout between John L. Sullivan and Jake Kilrain in Richburg, Mississippi. In this last legal bare-knuckle fight, Sullivan defeated Kilrain in the seventy-fifth round.

own. Boxing fans simply paid more attention to heavyweight championship bouts than to any other fights. (For additional information on the history of boxing, enter "boxing history" into any search engine and browse the sites listed.)

The electricity that surrounds a world heavyweight championship fight was first brought home to Clay when he happened to overhear a broadcast of such a match. He was all alone, walking to Stoner's gym, when he spotted a group of people clustered around a parked car whose radio was broadcasting a championship fight that was in progress. Clay went over to the car and elbowed a spot for himself next to a door so he could hear more clearly. The fight was a fierce contest, and the group huddled around the car was excited by it.

Suddenly, one of the boxers scored a knockout, and the fight was over. "The winner," the ringside announcer said, "and still heavyweight champion of the world, Rocky Marciano."

"And still heavyweight champion of the world . . ." These words rang magically in Clay's ears and left him without any doubts: He wanted to be a heavyweight, and someday he wanted to be the heavyweight champion. He asked Martin about his chances of becoming a heavyweight; Martin looked at the 112-pound fighter and just shook his head in amazement. Stoner had a different reaction. He told Clay that he had the raw skill to become a champion—perhaps not the heavyweight champion but nonetheless a champion in whatever weight division he would naturally belong to once he matured.

Clay first had to perfect his boxing technique, Stoner said. He needed to stop flailing about; he should concentrate on conserving his energy by throwing fewer but more accurate punches. Encouraged by the confidence Stoner expressed in his ability, Clay, under Stoner's guidance, began honing the techniques he would use throughout the rest of his career: He improved the quickness of his punches; he began to fight more defensively, moving and circling around in the ring to avoid his opponent; and, in what would eventually become his trademark, he learned the art of leaning back, throwing a quick jab, then simply bending or leaning backward so that his opponent would miss on the counterpunch.

KEEPING HIS EYES ON THE PRIZE

By 1958, Clay had improved his skills so much that he was able to win a berth in his first national Golden Gloves tournament, held in Chicago, Illinois. He had grown in size, too. At the age of 16, he had become a light heavyweight, weighing in at around 180 pounds. He did well in the tournament and won enough fights to make it past the semifinals, but he lost to another fighter in the final elimination round.

Dejected after his loss, Clay made his way back to the locker room. He was looking to have a conversation with some heavyweights to help take his mind off the defeat. He had the time to meet a few of them before he returned to Louisville.

In the locker room, Clay saw the Reverend Mr. Williams, a trainer from St. Louis, Missouri, whom he had met earlier in the week. He had developed a liking for the trainer partly because he managed only heavyweights. The Reverend Mr. Williams called them dinosaurs: They were so powerfully focused on their goals that they were always in danger of forgetting to think of anything but their opponents. According to the Reverend Mr. Williams, heavyweights were lumbering predators who were so highly attuned to devouring other dinosaurs that they were as feared as the *Tyrannosaurus rex*. Also like the king of the dinosaurs, their narrow focus always put them in danger of extinction.

Clay went over to the reverend to ask him where he could find some heavyweights. He had noticed the flyweights and the lightweights chattering to each other all week long, but the heavyweights had kept mostly to themselves.

The reverend was taping the hands of one of his fighters in preparation for a bout. His answer to Clay's request to meet some heavyweights was direct. "Heavyweights don't hibernate together," the reverend said.

Clay asked him what he meant by not hibernating together.

"Run together, hide out together, buddy together," the Reverend Mr. Williams said. "Dinosaurs don't do that."

But why not? Clay wanted to know.

"It's against the law of nature," the reverend said. "Everybody got buddies, I know. But not dinosaurs. The dinosaur is different. He's got his own satellite. His own crowd."

"Birds of a different feather flock together," Clay insisted.

"But birds of prey don't flock together. And dinosaurs are demons of prey," the reverend said, having the last word.

Clay did not say anything in response; he was beginning to learn a few things about heavyweights.

He returned to the Golden Gloves national tournament again in 1959 and 1960, winning the light-heavyweight championship both times. In 1960, he also won the Amateur Athletic Union championship and qualified as a light heavyweight for the U.S. Olympic boxing team. After another fighter distracted him by chattering in the ring during an Olympic trial bout, Clay picked up the habit, and it soon became one of his trademarks.

The 1960 Olympic Games were held in Rome, Italy—a fitting site for a young gladiator like Clay. Eighteen years old and very quick in and out of the ring, he was ready to show off his talent to the world. He advanced smoothly through the competition, and his talents were touted by the American television networks. For the first time in his career, millions of people in his own country and in other countries around the world got a good look at him. He was no longer a shy, awkward boy but a good-looking, likable, and talkative young man.

The championship bout in the 1960 Olympics was fought on September 5. Clay's opponent was a 23-year-old southpaw from Poland named Zbigniew Pietrzyskowski, a veteran of 230 fights. Clay had trouble at first against the more experienced left-handed fighter, but the young American gradually took control of the fight. He ended the bout by giving the Pole a tremendous battering in the last round, opening up a cut over Pietrzyskowski's left eye that made him vulnerable to Clay's right hook. The judges awarded Clay a unanimous 5–0 decision, which gave him the Olympic gold medal and the invaluable publicity that came with it.

TURNING PRO

Following his victory, Clay was at the top of the amateur boxing world. The next step for him was to become a professional boxer. Accordingly, serious courting by those who wanted to be his manager soon began.

At age 18, Clay qualified for the 1960 Olympics in Rome, Italy. He defeated the Polish boxer Zbigniew Pietrzyskowski to win the gold medal. Clay (middle) is seen here with fellow U.S. gold medal winners Wilbert McClure (left) and Edward Crook (right).

One of the most important decisions that every fighter has to make is whom to choose as the person or organization that will represent him in the business of boxing. The manager's role is crucial because he is the person who books opponents, chooses venues, and negotiates contracts with clubs and coliseums as well as radio and television networks. For making the decisions that guide a fighter's career, the manager receives a portion of the boxer's fee for a fight. Under the best of circumstances, the manager consults with the boxer about these decisions so that there is agreement between them, but many managers have tried to trick or bully a fighter—especially a young fighter—into signing unfair contracts or making other exploitative arrangements.

In the 1940s and 1950s, much of the fight business fell under the influence of organized crime. During that time, it was not unusual for a manager to demand that a fighter deliberately lose a match so that the racketeers could win large amounts of money by betting against the fighter. This type of match was known as a "fixed" fight, and it was only one of many ways that a manager who had made some sort of an arrangement with the criminal element could exploit a boxer. Because Clay was well aware of the pitfalls one could encounter when choosing a manager, he proceeded cautiously with his decision.

In the spring and summer before his Olympic victory, a wealthy Louisville businessman approached Clay through Martin. This businessman, William Reynolds, was an heir to the Reynolds Aluminum fortune. He had heard that Clay was a major contender for the Olympic gold medal, and he was interested in backing Clay—by becoming his manager—once he became a professional fighter. Because Reynolds was already rich, it is probable that his interest in Clay had as much to do with the prestige of backing a champion fighter as it did with accumulating more money.

Reynolds sought to entice Clay by employing him as a laborer around his luxurious Louisville home. He also bought Clay new equipment and promised him a large contract if he won the gold medal. Yet Reynolds never gave Clay the feeling that he cared for him as a person. It seemed to Clay that Reynolds wanted to own him as though he were a piece of property, and this was not the kind of relationship that the young fighter wanted. He was too aware of his people's history of slavery to allow any manager to feel as though he owned him.

Immediately after Clay won the gold medal in Rome, Reynolds lavished attention on the new champion. On Clay's way back to Louisville from Italy, Reynolds let him stay free of charge for a week at his suite in New York City's luxurious Waldorf-Astoria Hotel. He provided Clay with money to buy expensive presents for his parents, and he provided him with pocket money to spend around town.

One of the first things that Clay did with Reynolds's money was to look up Sugar Ray Robinson, who had recently retired from the ring and was running a nightclub in Harlem. The former welterweight and middleweight champion had been one of Clay's heroes for some time. The young champion introduced himself to the old pro and then asked him to be his manager. Robinson, apparently content with his life and only dimly aware of who Clay was, turned down the young Olympian's offer.

Shortly after this encounter, Clay returned home to a hero's welcome in Louisville. He was feted and saluted by the governor of Kentucky as well as by both the mayor and the police chief of Louisville. He was even given a parade down the main street of his hometown, but when he went to eat at a restaurant, he was refused service because he was black. He subsequently threw his Olympic gold medal into the Ohio River in disgust at the country he had represented at the Olympic Games.

Before long, Reynolds sent over his contract offer to manage Clay. So did former boxing champions Archie Moore and Rocky Marciano, the well-respected manager Cus D'Amato, and a group of 10 Louisville businessmen who called themselves the Louisville Millionaires. Clay and his father, with the assistance of a trusted family attorney, looked over all of the offers carefully. The two best offers were from Reynolds and the Louisville Millionaires.

There was scarcely any difference between the two contracts, but Clay had little difficulty in deciding which one to accept. He informed an angry Martin that he was turning down Reynolds's offer. This rejection ended Clay's relationship not only with Reynolds but with Martin, too.

The Louisville Millionaires were headed by Bill Faversham, the son of an English actor. Their contract with Clay ran for six years, from 1960 to 1966. They gave him a $10,000 advance, and in turn they were to receive 50 percent of his earnings—both in and out of the ring—for the duration of their agreement.

At the time, Clay felt lucky to have negotiated such a deal. He used the advance to pay off the mortgage of his parents' house and to repair its leaks and sagging porch. He also had the comfort of knowing that his managers were honest. They would stick to the agreement that the two parties had made; they would never ask him to deliberately lose a fight; and they would schedule him fairly, asking him to fight against equal and worthy opponents.

BECOMING A CONTENDER

Next, Clay had to select the best trainer that he could find. Stoner had been a fine trainer for Clay when he was still an amateur, but he did not have the ring experience that the fighter needed now that Clay had become a professional.

The Louisville group knew that Archie Moore ran a boxing camp in the hills above San Diego in southern California. Moore had the experience that Clay was looking for: He had been actively involved in boxing since 1938, and he had won the light-heavyweight championship in 1952, keeping the title for 10 years. By 1960, Moore was 47 years old and nearing the end of his boxing career, but he agreed to become Clay's trainer.

Moore's camp was in the country because he liked to isolate his fighters from distractions and temptations. He also felt that it was best to bring Clay along slowly toward the championship. Consequently, the young fighter was not allowed to spar with Moore himself until weeks after he had reported to the camp. Clay bridled at Moore's slow pace; he felt that he was ready to begin his climb to the top of the boxing world right away, and he pushed for a sparring session with the older fighter. (Sparring is when two boxers get into the ring to fight a practice round. Sparring rounds are usually three minutes long—the same length as a round in a regular boxing match. If a boxer wants to increase his stamina, he will spar for longer periods—sometimes up to seven or eight minutes a round.)

Clay finally succeeded in getting Moore into the ring with him, and the two fighters sparred for several rounds. Clay punched Moore all over the ring. He hit him with hooks, crosses, and uppercuts and generally took out his frustrations on Moore. After these rounds, Clay knew that he needed another trainer. Seeing how easily he handled the current light-heavyweight champion even if he was no longer in his prime convinced Clay that he was indeed ready to move ahead at a faster pace than Moore had suggested.

During the time that Clay spent in Moore's camp, he also learned that he could not train in isolation. He said:

> I decided that if I was going to be a fighter, I would have to train around people. I'd have to be around women and children, near barbershops, see people getting their shoes shined, watch the traffic, watch people go in and out of stores, hear them talk and talk back to them. And above all, I wanted to be associated with the instructor who would use his instructions on someone else. Not me. I had gone far past the training period. I wanted to fight, only to fight.

A full-blown heavyweight, Clay had indisputably become a dinosaur.

After leaving Moore's camp, Clay hooked up with a well-known trainer named Angelo Dundee, who had trained such top fighters as Carmen Basilio, Luis Rodriguez, and Willie Pastrano. Dundee knew how good Clay was, and he quickly agreed to take on the young contender. The trainer said of Clay, "He was always the first in and the last out of the gym."

With Dundee serving as his sounding board, Clay threw himself into the grinding tour of boxing that is typical of a hustling young professional. His first professional bout took place in Louisville on October 29, 1960. The result was a six-round decision over Tunney Hunsaker.

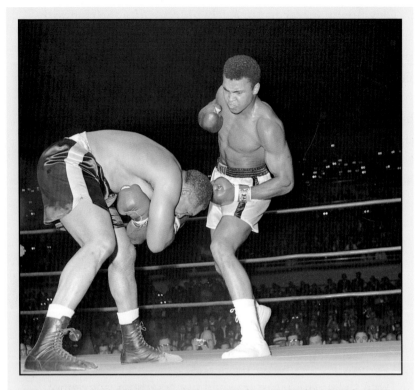

After turning pro, Clay chose former boxing champion Archie Moore
to be his trainer. However, Clay did not find Moore's techniques
challenging enough and after easily defeating the boxing champion
in sparring rounds he found a new trainer. In 1962, Clay defeated
Moore again with a knockout in his first public match, seen here.

Clay fought eight bouts in 1961 and six in 1962, averaging a
fight every seven weeks. He won all 14 of these fights, 12 of them
by knockouts. In 1962, he also appeared in a minor role in the
film version of Rod Setting's play *Requiem for a Heavyweight*.
One of the most interesting fights during this period in Clay's
career was his match with Moore, his former trainer, in
November 1962. Because they had once had a sparring session,
the fight was, in a sense, a rematch. It was also Clay's first public
match with a major fighter. The fight was televised, and Clay's
share, $45,000, was at the time by far his largest purse.

Because Clay had so easily dominated Moore two years before, when he was still a green young pro, he was confident that he would win the match. What made the fight even more significant to him was that the reigning heavyweight champion, Charles "Sonny" Liston, would be in the audience. As was becoming Clay's style, he composed a poem that predicted the outcome of the match. "They'll all fall in the round I call!" he maintained, and he said before the Moore fight:

When you come to the fight,
Don't block the halls,
And don't block the door,
For y'all may go home,
After round four.

The fight was held on the older fighter's home ground, in Los Angeles, California, and the crowd was wildly partisan. In spite of the fans, who were screaming to Moore, "Shut him up," and, "Hit him in the mouth," Clay methodically demolished his opponent in four rounds, just as he had predicted in his poem.

An intriguing encounter occurred in Clay's dressing room after the fight. Amid the laughter and joking of Clay's entourage, Liston walked into the room to meet the new contender. Clay looked at his chief rival, who was known for his ice-cold stare, and proclaimed:

King Liston will stay,
Only until he meets Cassius Clay.
Moore fell in four,
Liston in eight.

Liston just glared at Clay. The reigning champion then said, "You go eight seconds with me, little boy, and I'll give you the title."

4

A Call From Islam

During Clay's next three fights in 1963, he strove to perfect the antics that would make him stand out in the crowded field of heavyweight contenders. While he continued to predict, with his own style of poetry, the round in which he would knock out his opponent, he also performed some new publicity stunts. Traveling outside the United States for the first time as a professional, he went to England to fight the British heavyweight champion, Henry Cooper. Before the fight, Clay donned a crown and cape and declared himself "the uncrowned king of heavyweights." He also predicted that he would knock out Cooper in the fifth round. The English fans flocked to see Clay get his comeuppance, only to watch Cooper fall in the sixth round.

Clay's campaign to seek recognition for himself worked. The more he bragged, strutted, and spouted his poetry, the more he stirred up the boxing world and an aroused boxing world always means more money for a boxer. This was one of the main reasons for Clay's theatrics.

After the Cooper fight, Jack Nilon, Liston's manager, stopped by Clay's dressing room with the news that Liston had decided to fight Clay. Nilon also said that he had a message to deliver from the champion to Clay: He should "drink [his] orange juice and milk shakes" and "stay well for the fight." Clay, who had recently married Sonji Roi, should not stay up late worrying about the outcome of the moneymaking fight because, according to Liston, "now your wife can be a rich widow." The match was set for February 25, 1964, in Miami, Florida.

WILD SELF-PROMOTION

Liston's offer to fight Clay was proof that the young challenger had gained enough notoriety for himself to grab the champion's undivided attention. In the months before his fight with Cooper in England, Clay had stalked Liston across the United States. In Las Vegas, Nevada, shortly before Liston was scheduled to fight Floyd Patterson, Clay had disrupted a blackjack game in which Liston was playing by yelling that he, Clay, was the real champ—the man who would put Liston to the ultimate test. Liston, having been tipped off about Clay, then pulled a pistol from his jacket and fired it several times in Clay's direction, which sent Clay running for his life through the casino hall. Even Clay was amused when he found out later that the shots had been blanks.

A few weeks after the showdown in the casino, Clay again tweaked the champion by showing up outside Liston's house in Denver, Colorado, early one morning, screaming how he wanted to "whip the champ" then and there in his front yard. Liston came out of his house, and the police arrived just as he was smashing in the windows of Clay's bus. The next day, many of the nation's major papers carried stories about the incident—as Clay had hoped they would.

Besides attracting publicity, Clay's antics also served another of the challenger's goals. They presumably made Liston wonder about Clay's sanity. Clay felt that the champion might lose a bit of his confidence and concentration if he spent part of his time brooding about the mental health of his opponent. Sometimes all that a boxer needs to give himself an advantage in an important fight is to cause a minor lapse in his opponent's mental preparation.

During the months that Clay had been dashing around the country, bewildering and intriguing people with his curious behavior, he had also quietly begun studying the precepts of the religion of Islam and meeting with representatives of a black American religious group called the Lost-Found Nation of Islam. Founded in 1931 by Elijah Muhammad, the group follows a philosophy that is largely based on the teachings of Muhammad, the seventh-century founder of the religion of Islam. The Nation of Islam also preaches the doctrine of independence and self-help for black Americans.

RELIGIOUS CHANGE

In the early 1960s, the Nation of Islam advocated total separation of black and white Americans. The group, whose members are called Black Muslims, labeled whites as "devils" who were responsible for the plight of blacks all around the world. The Black Muslims suggested that the states of Mississippi and Alabama be partitioned off from the United States as an independent nation for blacks who were then living in America. The preachers of the Nation of Islam also insisted that members of their mosques drop their surnames, which they pointed out were not the original names of their ancestors from Africa but the names of slave owners, and adopt instead the letter X, which would stand for their lost African name or some appropriate Muslim name.

Thus, in the summer of 1963, Clay more or less secretly changed his name—first to Cassius X and then to Muhammad Ali.

Publicly, he was still known as Cassius Clay. To his Black Muslim brothers and sisters, he was known as Muhammad Ali.

Ali subsequently hired several Muslims to join his entourage. He took on Captain Samuels, the leader of the Miami mosque of the Nation of Islam, as his security chief and bodyguard, and he retained the services of several Muslim women to cook the careful and restricted diet that is required of all followers of the Nation of Islam. He also forswore the use of alcohol, coffee, cigarettes, and all nonmedicinal drugs.

Ali had good reason to keep his conversion to Islam a secret: Racial tensions in America in the 1960s were reaching a breaking point. As members of civil rights groups pressed their demands for racial justice and equality in the South, their demands were officially met by attacks from the police and, unofficially, by violence from white racists; elsewhere, the black ghettos of most big cities were seething with tension.

The Nation of Islam was then one of the most radical of the black groups demanding change. Spurred on by Malcolm X, who had become one of the group's most vigorous leaders, the Black Muslim movement was attracting an increasing number of converts in the major cities of America. It was also attracting much criticism for its views on race relations.

Three days before Ali's championship match with Liston, Bill McDonald, the promoter of the fight, learned of Ali's association with the Black Muslims. Malcolm X had visited Ali's gym in Miami, and newspapers in New York had carried articles about Ali's visit to a Muslim mosque in Harlem. Claiming that Ali's conversion to Islam was bad publicity for the fight and could cause him to lose the money he had invested in promoting the fight, McDonald demanded that Ali make a public statement disavowing support for the Nation of Islam. Ali refused to do this, so McDonald tried to cancel the fight. A day of tense confrontations between the white promoter and the black challenger followed. The reluctant promoter was persuaded to let the fight go on only

In 1963, Cassius Clay joined the Nation of Islam and changed his name to Muhammad Ali. Once word of his conversion to the controversial religion spread, he received criticism and death threats, but he remained a committed Muslim. Here, in 1968, Ali addresses a gathering of Black Muslims in Chicago with Nation of Islam leader Elijah Muhammad looking on.

after hours of wrangling with Ali's trainer, Angelo Dundee, and his managers, the Louisville Millionaires.

RUN FOR THE HEAVYWEIGHT CHAMPIONSHIP BELT

As the time for Ali's first heavyweight championship bout drew closer, he had another problem to worry about in addition to McDonald's threat to cancel the fight. He had begun to receive threatening phone calls from people who had learned of his conversion to Islam and disapproved of his outrageous behavior. Racial slurs and death threats were hurled at him. He was told that no matter what he might do in the ring, he would not win the fight.

Ali became extremely cautious, even with those who were helping him train. He knew that two ways to defeat a boxer were to poison the water he drank between rounds and to put an astringent substance that would affect his vision into the water that was used to wipe his face between rounds. Consequently, Ali allowed only Muslims to handle these chores; even Angelo Dundee, who would remain with Ali throughout his career, was prohibited from doing them.

The title bout began with Ali, still known to most of the world as Cassius Clay, and Liston facing each other in the ring as the referee gave them instructions. Ali talked through his mouthpiece to Liston, who, as he usually did just before a fight was about to begin, silently stared at his opponent. A former union strongman, Liston was big and tough. His wrists were as large as most men's calves, and he was one of the hardest punchers in all of boxing.

Looking for a quick knockout, Liston charged Ali in the first round, relentlessly stalking him around the ring. Sometimes Liston even ran right at him to deliver his ferocious round-house punches, which Ali neatly sidestepped or avoided by using a trick he had discovered at Stoner's Louisville gym: He would lean away from an oncoming punch at the last possible moment, and the punch would harmlessly whiz by his face.

Ali did not throw many punches until he had gauged Liston's strategy, which was to score a knockout as early as possible. In the latter part of the first round, Ali began to hit Liston with quick, precise jabs that snapped the champion's head around.

The second and third rounds continued in the same way, with Liston swinging wildly, trying for a knockout, and Ali dancing and darting around the ring, never getting hit hard while lacing Liston with jabs that began to dull the champion's reactions. Suddenly, near the end of the third round, Ali hit his opponent with a glancing shot to the head that opened a cut under Liston's left eye. Liston had never been cut before, and he began to panic once he realized what had happened to him.

Liston was not used to going beyond three or four rounds; in most of his fights, he had knocked out his opponent before the fifth round. As the fourth round took place, the champion began to tire. Knowing that his energy was waning and that the cut under his eye, which had been treated between rounds, could be reopened at any time, he desperately continued to press his assault against Ali. Ali was maddeningly difficult to catch and hit. He danced and circled around Liston and started talking to the older man more and more, taunting him.

During the fourth round, Liston pulled a muscle in his shoulder while throwing a desperation punch at Ali. When the round was over, Liston's trainer rubbed the fighter's shoulder with liniment to keep the muscle from tightening up. The medication got into Ali's eyes in the fifth round as the two fighters clinched. Fearing that Liston's gloves had been doctored with the liniment, Ali stumbled around the ring, literally holding off Liston at arm's length. When Ali returned to his corner at the end of the fifth round, he insisted that Dundee stop the fight and have Liston's gloves examined. Instead of stopping the fight, the shrewd Dundee calmed down his fighter. He told Ali that he had come too far to stop now; he must get back into the ring and beat Liston.

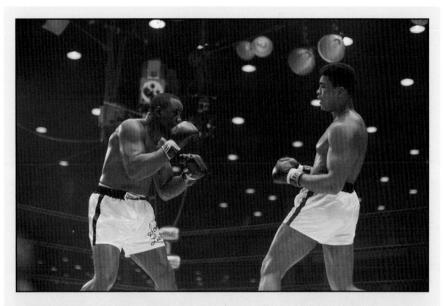

In the months leading up to his title bout with reigning world champion Sonny Liston, Ali gained notoriety with his outrageous statements and antics. But in the ring during the February 1964 fight, seen here, he was all business, sidestepping Liston's wild punches and attempts at a knockout.

Ali's eyesight slowly cleared up in the sixth round. Liston, however, was still having his troubles. He was breathing heavily, his energy was spent, and he could not punch well with his damaged arm. Ali hit him with some more hard shots to the head before the round ended. He was giving substance to the slogan that Drew "Bundini" Brown had recently come up with for Ali: "Float like a butterfly, sting like a bee."

When the bell rang for the start of the seventh round, an astonishing thing happened: Liston sat sulking on his stool in his corner; he would not come into the ring. The fight was over! Ali saw his trainers and cornermen throw up their hands and heard them shout with joy as they rushed into the ring. Then he heard an announcement that was similar to those sweet words that he remembered coming from a car radio on

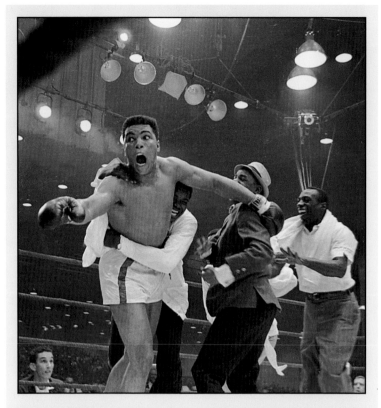

Ali defeated Sonny Liston on a seventh round technical knockout to become the heavyweight champion of the world. Ali's handlers had to hold him back as he exuberantly celebrated the announcement.

the streets of Louisville: "Ladies and gentlemen, the new heavyweight champion of the world . . ."

FROM CLAY TO ALI

The day after the fight, Ali publicly announced his conversion to Islam and the change in his name. The new champion then took some time off from boxing. He visited Africa and the Middle East, and he began granting interviews to the major papers of the world and making appearances on American television. Many who were not boxing fans soon grew familiar with Ali.

It was not too long before Ali returned to the ring—the ring was not only his paycheck; it was his life as well. Besides his need to box, he craved the adulation of his fans and the exaltation that came with fame and success. A rematch with Liston was scheduled for May 25, 1965, in Lewiston, Maine.

Ali's personal triumph was diminished somewhat by several events that took place between the first and second fights with Liston. In 1964, shortly after Ali won the heavyweight title, Malcolm X broke rank with the Nation of Islam and formed his own religious and political groups dedicated to spiritual enlightenment and social justice. A feud quickly developed between the followers of Elijah Muhammad and those who left the Nation of Islam to join Malcolm X. Ali chose to remain loyal to the Nation of Islam even though he admired Malcolm X.

In February 1965, Malcolm X was assassinated in New York City. Two of those charged with his murder were Black Muslims from the New Jersey mosque of the Nation of Islam. As Ali trained for his rematch with Liston, he not only received the usual threatening calls from white racists; he also received death threats from people who claimed to be followers of Malcolm X. Ali was subsequently guarded by the FBI and the local police during the month and a half that preceded the fight.

Just as Ali was facing danger due to his religious life, his personal life grew troubled as well: His marriage to Sonji was beginning to come apart. Because his wife was not interested in Islam, she refused to stop smoking and wearing makeup. Nor did she want to wear the austere clothing that women are required to wear by the Nation of Islam. The night before his fight with Liston, Ali and Sonji agreed to get a divorce.

Because of these crises and distractions, Ali's concentration was not totally focused on his opponent when he stepped into the ring to fight Liston for the second time. Ali spared himself from facing a long and punishing fight, which he might have lost. In the first round, he hit Liston with what looked like a weak punch, and the man whom Ali had labeled "the big, ugly bear" crumpled to the mat. He stayed down for the count; when he finally got up, he appeared more than a little bit dazed. Ali had beaten Liston for the second—and last—time.

Many sportswriters were uncertain about exactly what took place during the fight. It seemed to them that Ali had finished off Liston too quickly, too easily. Suspicions circulated that the fight had been fixed. Tape replays of the fight show that Liston was hit solidly by a fast punch. Just how hard the punch was and how hard it jarred him, no one but Liston can say.

Ali had only one more fight in 1965, with former heavyweight champion Floyd Patterson, a gutsy fighter whose personality was the opposite of Ali's. Whereas Ali was loud and extravagant, Patterson was quiet and dignified. Ali, after refusing to renounce the Nation of Islam, had become one of America's most visible symbols of black pride. Patterson was not a leading figure in the struggle for racial equality (although he was clearly involved in the struggle). The mainstream press, which was controlled mostly by whites, was cheering for Patterson to take the title away from Ali. Reacting to their favoritism, Ali labeled Patterson as a "black white hope," alluding to the days in the early 1900s when a number of white fighters tried to take away the heavyweight title from Jack Johnson, the first black world champion. On November 11 in Las Vegas, Patterson fought bravely for 12 rounds until Ali battered him into submission.

In 1966, Ali's contract with the Louisville Millionaires expired and he took on a new manager, Herbert Muhammad, the son of the founder of the Nation of Islam, Elijah Muhammad. Ali's earnings rose significantly with Herbert Muhammad as his manager. In his first three fights under Muhammad, Ali earned an average of $420,000 per fight—much more than he had been making with his former managers.

In the two years that followed the Patterson fight, Ali fought every major heavyweight contender and beat them, all, mostly by knockouts. By 1967, he had virtually run out of opponents. He was in peak form. Nothing, it seemed, could stop Ali from becoming the greatest heavyweight champion of all time.

5

A Technical Knockout

Just when the goals that Ali had worked so hard for had been reached and his life seemed to be in almost perfect order, unforeseen events conspired to shatter his sense of harmony and success. His initial confrontation with such trouble came in 1964, in the form of a notice from the U.S. Selective Service Board, which he received just before his first fight with Liston. The young fighter ignored the notice that he was to attend an entrance examination for the army. Ali, who was then 22 years old, had been obtaining postponements of this examination since his 18th birthday. These postponements had been arranged by his influential managers, the Louisville Millionaires, who had wanted to see him make as much money as he could before his induction into the army.

The summons from the Selective Service Board ordered Ali to appear at the board's office in Miami so that his draft status could be judged by board officials. Beginning in the early 1950s, the United States manned its armed forces by means of a system called the universal military draft. According to this system, all young men were required by law to join a branch of the armed forces soon after their 18th birthday or graduation from high school. Under certain circumstances, a young man such as Ali could delay his entrance into the army for a few years. The draft, however, was a federal institution that every young American male had to reckon with sooner or later.

The draft was made "universal" so that the burden of defending the country would be shared equally by all ethnic, religious, and social groups. At least this was how the system was ideally supposed to work. In reality, many people were exempted from the draft: those who were mentally, emotionally, or physically incapable of service; those with families to support; and those who were studying at a college or a university. (For additional information on draft procedures, enter "Vietnam draft" or "selective service" into any search engine and browse the sites listed.)

The summons from the Selective Service Board was particularly worrisome to Ali because his induction into the army would disrupt his professional career for at least two years. Other well-known fighters had been called to serve in the armed forces before Ali. The most notable example was the heavyweight champion Joe Louis, who served in the army during World War II. As a celebrated boxer, Louis served a ceremonial tour of duty. He was not sent to the battlefront; instead, he was asked to visit bases and hospitals both in the United States and abroad.

Ali knew that he would be drafted sooner or later because he did not qualify for an exemption from the draft; although he had a wife to support, the large amounts of money he had been making disqualified him from obtaining an exemption so he could provide for his family. Yet he had been given assurances that when he was eventually drafted into the army,

Ali was first summoned by the Selective Service Board to join the army in 1964. He refused to join because he opposed the Vietnam War, a stance that caused an uproar across the country. Here, Ali is interviewed outside the Army Induction Center in Houston, Texas, in 1967.

he would not be sent to Vietnam as a combat soldier. Instead, his stint would be along the lines of Louis's. After all, Ali, too, was a celebrated boxer.

Conscience and his Muslim beliefs were causing him to consider refusing induction into the army because he was politically and morally opposed to America's increasing involvement in the Vietnam War. As a member of the Nation of Islam, he believed (with a few exceptions) that the taking of life in warfare was not morally justifiable. He also believed that the government and the people of the United States should not be involved in what Elijah Muhammad called "a fight inside the Vietnamese's own family."

The members of the Nation of Islam also felt that black Americans were "subject peoples" within their own country. Consequently, they should not be asked to fight another non-Caucasian group—in this case, the Vietnamese. Believing that the Vietnam War marked the domination of a foreign race by the white American ruling class, the Black Muslims maintained that such a fight was the responsibility of whites only.

Ali and the Nation of Islam were not alone in holding these views. By 1964, many young Americans from all different racial backgrounds strongly disagreed with the the country's policy in Southeast Asia—and many of them, like Ali, were willing to express their disagreement by refusing induction into the army. In doing so, they risked a prison sentence of five years or the possibility of a long exile if they chose to avoid the draft by leaving the country.

Ali eventually flunked the intelligence test of the Selective Service examination because he did not answer a number of the questions. He claimed that he had left some of the responses blank because he did not know the answers to the questions and was reluctant to risk a guess. Others thought differently of his actions, which resulted in him receiving a temporary deferment from the army. Congressman Mendel Rivers of South Carolina stated:

> Clay's deferment is an insult to every mother's son serving in Vietnam. Here he is, smart enough to finish high school, write his kind of poetry, promote himself all over the world, make a million a year, drive around in red Cadillacs—and they say he's too dumb to tote a gun. Who's dumb enough to believe that?

Such an outcry not only showed the congressman's contempt for Ali but indicated little appreciation for the feeling of resentment against the war that was growing throughout the United States.

NO TO WAR

In fact, the antiwar movement represented just one of many great changes that were sweeping the nation in the 1960s. The civil rights movement, which attacked racism through large-scale demonstrations, changed forever the relations between black and white Americans. America's youth, quiet and conformist through the 1950s, suddenly became noisy and critical of the flaws in American society and culture in the 1960s. Rock and roll became the music of youthful protest and celebration. The birth control pill, widely available for the first time in the early 1960s, heralded a new era of sexual freedom. Old and established moral certainties were being challenged everywhere. Yet it was the Vietnam War more than anything else that symbolized to a generation of rebellious Americans what had gone wrong with their country.

By 1967, Americans no longer saw the conflict in Vietnam as a minor skirmish at the edge of the civilized world. The U.S. government was spending $2 billion a month on the war and had 450,000 troops stationed in Vietnam. Every week almost 100 American soldiers died fighting in Vietnam and more than 500 were wounded. Most crucial to the making of public opinion, this drama of human suffering was broadcast every night via television into the homes of millions of Americans.

Mass resistance against an unpopular war was not an entirely new phenomenon in American history; it had occurred at the beginning of the Civil War nearly a century before. Resistance to a war and refusal of induction on such a large scale was new to twentieth-century America, however, and it caused resentment and bitterness between three generations of Americans: On one side of this conflict were the veterans of World War I and those who had willingly fought in World War II, and on the other side were their sons and grandsons, who did not want to fight the Vietcong in Vietnam.

Ali was not alone in his opposition to the war and the universal draft. Ali is seen here in Louisville, Kentucky, with Martin Luther King, Jr., conferring about Ali's court suit to prevent his Army induction.

GROWING IN POPULARITY

Although Ali was caught in the middle of this conflict, his life in the mid-1960s was not entirely filled with confrontation. He loved the camera, and the camera treated him favorably in return. People around the world responded warmly to his sincerity and to his obvious love of children, even if at times they were baffled by his wilder antics.

To many in America, Ali seemed to be a new kind of black man—one who either delighted or horrified his audience, depending on their beliefs and cultural background. He was utterly confident (even cocky), articulate, assertive, and in turn playful and serious. He was always challenging conventional wisdom and authority. With the possible exception of the Brazilian soccer star Pelé, he was the most popular sports figure on earth in the mid-1960s.

By 1967, Ali had been the undisputed heavyweight champion for three years, and he had gone beyond the confines of boxing to become a media celebrity. His words and deeds had been denounced and encouraged, explained and analyzed, in every major language of the world. Every other week, it seemed, he had a new prediction in verse about the state of the world or the fate of his next opponent in the ring.

Ali loved his star status and went out of his way to stir up controversy. He courted other celebrities and notable figures—persons as diverse as the popular wrestler Gorgeous George and the British mathematician and philosopher Bertrand Russell. Ali's media whirligigs always had a point: They drew people to his fights and increased his purse—the money he could demand for his performance in the ring.

In many ways, Ali was a creature of his age. At a time when the influential artistic movement known as pop (which was short for "popular") art was combining high and low culture, the comical and the serious, so was Ali. A clear example of his "pop" sensibility took place on a television talk show in 1965. Ali spoke about his upcoming fight with

Patterson, then read some of his poetry while the flamboyant entertainer Liberace played a piano in the background. Ali's poetry began:

> It all started twenty years past,
> The Greatest of them All was born at last.
> The very first words from his Louisville lips
> "I'm pretty as a picture and there's no one I can't whip."

FOLLOWING HIS CONSCIENCE

Although Ali often displayed his comic side to the public, he could also be quite serious about his beliefs and very stubborn in defending them. As America's involvement in Vietnam wore on, Ali needed these qualities to face the difficult times that lay ahead.

Until 1966, Ali's status in the files of the Selective Service Board remained classified as 1-Y, the designation given to those who had failed either the physical or written part of the Selective Service examination. In February 1966, however, new regulations lowered the requirements of the army draft. This caused Ali's hometown draft board to change his status to 1-A, making him a suitable candidate for service in the armed forces.

Ali was informed of the change in his draft status while he was in training for the third defense of his title. He responded with a stanza of impromptu poetry:

> Keep asking me, no matter how long
> On the war in Vietnam, I sing this song
> I ain't got no quarrel with the Viet Cong ...

His commitment to Islam had created uproar a year ago. This present bit of doggerel, broadcast that very evening on television news programs around the country, kicked up a storm at least equal to the prior controversy. While fan support on one hand countered by terrorizing threats on the other spun in, the good boy his family knew filed for status as a conscientious objector. Ali's anti-war stance poured fuel on the fire that eventually led to him being banned from professional boxing.

The first state of note that prohibited him from boxing was Illinois. Before his remark about the Vietcong, Ali had been scheduled to defend his title in Chicago against Ernie Terrell. Yet several weeks after Ali recited the Vietcong poem, the Illinois Boxing Commission demanded that he come before them to disavow what he had said. Ali appeared before the commission, but he would not apologize. The commission then refused him the right to fight in Illinois. The Terrell fight was canceled (it was later held in Houston, on February 6, 1967), and Ali in 1966 was forced to schedule all of his fights but one in foreign cities: He fought and beat George Chuvalo in Toronto, Canada, Henry Cooper and Brian London in London, England, and Karl Mildenberger in Frankfurt, West Germany; he defeated Cleveland Williams in Houston.

His Selective Service case had been referred to the FBI for investigation. Once the Bureau's review was completed, another selective service hearing was conducted in Louisville. The hearing officer concluded Ali was sincere in his religious objections to joining the U.S. Army and recommended sustaining his conscientious objector claim. The Department of Justice had other unfortunate ideas and requested maintaining Ali's service ready classification because he did not meet the three basic tests for a conscientious objector. That advice in hand, the service board denied his petition without providing a reason.

While the sport's ban was taking place, Robert Arum, the fighter's long-time business attorney, was joined by a host of lawyers, who rallied a defense that among other things charged the Selective Service Board with systemic racial bias. These attorneys included Chauncey Eskridge, who worked with Martin Luther King, Jr., and was quite familiar with civil rights

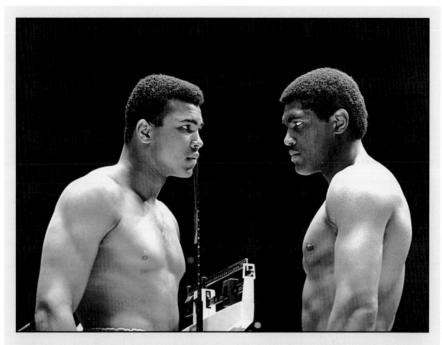

Illinois was followed by many other states in banning Ali from boxing due to his anti-war statements and draft evasion. Throughout 1966 almost all his fights were in foreign cities, and he was forced to cancel a fight against Ernie Terrell to defend his title. The match was rescheduled for February 1967, in Houston, and Ali is seen here with Terrell during a prefight weigh-in.

cases, along with Jack Greenberg, James M. Nabrit III, Jonathan Shapiro, and Elizabeth B. DuBois. This core group collaborated with a variety of lawyers to shape a series of appeals to the service boards and courts.

General Lewis B. Hershey, the National Director of Selective Service, interceded with two written requests to reopen the case, as appeals were being exhausted in Kentucky and Texas. The resulting examinations upheld the 1-A classification. Following more failed petitions, Ali's legal team acted to change the location of his draft induction from Louisville to Houston, in hope of finding more sympathetic treatment during the inevitable court battle. Their optimism proved unfounded. Ali, true to his word, refused induction inside the courthouse in Houston. For this act of defiance, he was pronounced guilty of draft evasion by an all-white jury. The district judge handed out the maximum sentence of a five-year jail term and $10,000 fine on June 20, 1967.

Ali's attorneys began court appeals to overturn the conviction. During this period, the champ remained free on bail. The boxing lockout started by the Illinois Boxing Commission continued throughout the country, until Ali was banned from fighting in every state. The state of New York, along with several other states, revoked his boxing license, and the World Boxing Association (WBA) stripped him of his world heavyweight championship title.

Unable to practice his profession, he found it difficult to earn a living. For a while, he was not allowed even to leave the country because the government had revoked his passport; the government insisted that he had to remain in the United States until his court case was resolved. Ali was convinced that he had done the right thing and that someday the righteousness of his beliefs would prevail. For the time being, though, he had no choice but to carry on while seeking strength and understanding in the words of his spiritual leader, Elijah Muhammad:

> Of this grief you and I must suffer, all these burdens we must bear.... I have no alternative than to tell you that there is not any life beyond the grave. There is no justice in the sweet bye and bye. Immortality is NOW, HERE. We are the blessed of God and we must exert every means to protect ourselves.

Ali did not know how long it would be before he was able to resume his boxing career. Yet throughout this period of being banned, which he called "the Exile," he drew on the teachings of the Nation of Islam and never gave in to despair.

6

The Exile

On the night of March 22, 1967, Ali fought Zora Foley at Madison Square Garden in New York City. It was a relatively uneventful evening for the champion. He easily handled Foley, and the fight ended with the challenger being knocked out in the seventh round. Because Foley was just one of many challengers in the secondary rank of heavyweight boxing, this fight was not a particularly important test for Ali. Nonetheless, the Foley fight would prove to be significant. Although Ali did not know it at the time, the bout would be his last professional fight for more than three years.

After Ali was convicted of draft evasion, he faced two immediate problems of equal importance: earning a living for himself outside of boxing and adopting a legal strategy that would keep him out of jail and eventually exonerate him. In confronting both of these problems, he sought the support and counsel of the Nation of Islam. Ali's closest adviser was his manager, Herbert Muhammad.

During the six years that Ali was affiliated with the Louisville Millionaires, he earned about $2 million. In the year before his ban from boxing, under Muhammad's management, he earned another $1.2 million. A large portion of this money went to his seconds and paid hotel and travel expenses for Ali's entourage, which was always a sizable group.

Despite high expenses, Ali had invested almost $100,000 of his money into a retirement fund. Following the advice of Muhammad, he had also invested in several small Muslim-owned businesses. The income that he earned from these investments helped to sustain him, but by themselves they were not enough to cover all of his costs.

In 1967, Ali was married to Belinda Boyd (who took the Muslim name of Kalilah Tolona). In early 1968, their first child was born. His growing family (he had four children with his second wife) naturally increased his financial obligations, which included substantial alimony payments to his former wife, Sonji Roi. He also had to pay for the full-time services of the team of lawyers who were appealing the conviction on draft evasion.

A former government prosecutor and budding fight promoter who worked with Ali, Arum was publicly confident about his client's chances of winning a ruling against the decision laid down by the federal court in Houston. Ali's appeal would take place in New Orleans. The location of the appeal and the public climate at the time of the appeal were crucial to success in cases similar to his. Although the appeals court could not be chosen by his defense attorneys, they had aligned their fate with the fifth circuit court when Ali's induction was transferred from Louisville to Houston.

BATTLING THE COURTS

The first appeals court to rule on Ali's case was the Federal Court of Appeals in New Orleans, Louisiana. One of the reasons

In the midst of his legal battles and ban from boxing, Ali married Belinda Boyd on August 19, 1967. Boyd, Ali's second wife, was a Black Muslim like Ali, and by 1968 they had their first child.

Ali and his legal staff had shifted the site of his military hearing from Louisville to a Houston courthouse was because the latter city was noted for having a fairly liberal court at that time. The New Orleans court ruled against Ali. After several failed petitions, his lawyers had no other choice if they wanted the conviction set aside but to take the case to the country's highest legal forum, the U.S. Supreme Court.

Arum knew that the federal courts, like other branches of the government, were susceptible to shifts in public opinion. Although such courts seemed to be removed from politics, their judges read newspapers and watched television just like everyone else. Accordingly, like everyone else, their ideas and opinions were subject to change. Because the timing of an appeal could be so important to the outcome, the appeal process for Ali was extraordinarily drawn out.

Ali raised the money for his legal defense and met other financial obligations with the assistance of Muhammad. They improvised an ingenious plan. Ali converted his popularity—especially among the nation's youth—into money: He became a paid speaker on the college lecture circuit. In December 1969, he appeared in a Broadway musical by Oscar Brown, Jr., called *Big Time Buck White*, and he also made frequent appearances on American radio and television talk shows. He even persuaded a major book publisher to sign him to a contract for his autobiography, entitled *The Greatest: My Own Story*. The book was eventually published in 1975.

OUTSIDE BOXING LOOKING IN

The college lecture circuit was the most rewarding of Ali's ventures during his exile from boxing. He had always been sociable—a fighter who fancied himself a man of the people and who loved to mix with all kinds of persons. Yet even Ali was surprised to discover how much of a hero he had become to the college youth of the 1960s.

Ali was buoyed by the support he found on college campuses, and his meetings with students as well as faculty members impressed upon him that he was far from alone in his struggle against the Vietnam War. People who came from vastly different backgrounds than his own congratulated him on his stand and offered him their aid. Encouragement from such an

In the late 1960s, Ali used his popularity to earn money to cover his legal fees and other financial obligations while he was unable to box. He gave lectures, appeared on talk shows, signed a book deal, and even appeared on Broadway. Here, Ali waits in costume to make his Broadway debut in the musical *Big Time Buck White*.

unexpected quarter gave Ali good reason to hope for the nation as well as for himself. He felt that perhaps the racial and social antagonisms that racked the country could be overcome, after all.

This feeling of hopefulness was diminished somewhat on April 4, 1968, when Martin Luther King, Jr., the nation's foremost civil rights leader and Ali's friend, was assassinated in Memphis, Tennessee. King's assassination set off riots in the black ghettos of more than a half-dozen American cities; the smoke from the burning ghettos of Washington, D.C., could be

Ali excelled on the college lecture circuit and found the venture very rewarding. He was happy to learn that he was admired and respected on college campuses, and the students gave him hope that the country could overcome its social problems. Here, Ali greets enthusiastic students after a 1968 rally on the St. John's University campus.

seen from the steps of the Capitol building. The assassination and the ensuing riots served to remind Americans that, in the words of the Report of the National Advisory Commission on Civil Disorders, the nation was still composed of "two societies, one black, one white—separate and unequal."

In this unequal American society, Ali was arrested and sentenced to ten days in a Dade County, Florida, jail for the minor infraction of driving without a valid license. Inside prison, he got an unforgettable taste of how tough the five-year sentence hanging over him could be, and it could be made worst by the world outside moving forward without him. In some ways it already had.

The sport of boxing did not stand still with Ali's departure from the scene. A dozen or so young heavyweights pursued the vacated title, and the two major world boxing organizations— the WBA and the World Boxing Council (WBC)—recognized a number of pretenders to Ali's throne. In time, a clearer picture of the major contenders emerged.

Jimmy Ellis, a childhood friend of Ali's as well as a former sparring partner, was the first to lay claim to the title. Not surprisingly, he had a boxing style that was remarkably similar to Ali's. Ellis was a defensive fighter—a boxer in the truest sense of the word. He knew all of the tricks that were required of a polished boxer, including how and when to feint, clinch, and cover up. He lacked two of Ali's main attributes: speed and stamina. These deficiencies left Ellis vulnerable when he met another heavyweight contender, Joe Frazier.

Formerly a meat packer from Philadelphia, Pennsylvania, Frazier was the archetypal journeyman boxer. There was nothing fancy about his style of boxing; he was a slugger with a steel chin who challenged his opponents with a relentless attack.

IN HIS OWN WORDS...

Ali spoke to author Thomas Hauser about his Dade County arrest and potential longer incarceration for draft evasion:

Jail is a bad place. I was there for about a week until they let us out for Christmas, and it was terrible. You're all locked up; you can't get out. The food is bad, and there's nothing good to do. You look out the window at cars and people, and everyone else seems so free. Little things you take for granted like sleeping good or walking down the street, you can't do them no more. A man's got to be real serious about what he believes to say he'll do that for five years, but I was ready if I had to go.

Frazier had a difficult climb to the top of the boxing world. Because he did not have an Olympic gold medal, he had to fight countless low-paying matches against little-known opponents in order to get a shot at the heavyweight crown.

By 1969, Frazier and Ellis had secured the heavyweight titles of the two major world boxing organizations: Frazier was recognized as WBA champ; Ellis claimed the WBC title. On February 16, 1970, Frazier beat Ellis to become—in Ali's absence—the undisputed heavyweight champion of the world.

Three other contenders played important roles in the heavyweight boxing scene from 1970 to 1975. George Chuvalo was a big and extremely strong heavyweight. He fought and lost a championship bout to Ali on March 29, 1966, and appeared in several more championship matches in the early 1970s. He never managed to win the undisputed championship title. Jerry Quarry, a Californian of Irish descent, was the major white heavyweight of the early 1970s. The other major contender to make his appearance during Ali's exile was George Foreman.

A native of Houston, Foreman followed much the same route that Ali did when he ascended to the top of the heavy-weight division. Like Ali, Foreman won an Olympic gold medal as a heavyweight in the 1968 games held in Mexico City, Mexico. Unlike Ali, Foreman was loudly patriotic. After Foreman's medal-winning victory in the Olympics, he paraded around the ring waving a tiny American flag.

It was not easy for Ali to remain inactive while other boxers jockeyed for the title he had once held. He was in the prime of his career as a fighter during this period of exile: When Frazier won the undisputed heavyweight championship in 1970, Ali was just turning 28 years old. He knew that if there had not been a war or if he had joined the army, he probably still would have been the champion, not Frazier.

Instead, the only boxing match in which Ali was allowed to participate was a staged fantasy bout between himself and the former heavyweight champion of the 1950s, Rocky Marciano. This fake fight, put together by a television production company in a Miami studio over a period of several days, was supposed to demonstrate what would have been the outcome if there had actually been an Ali–Marciano fight. It was the highlight of a series of "dream fights" between boxers who had never actually met in the ring. The fights were billed as being judged by a computer—a neat showman's trick that lent an air of bogus impartiality to the enterprise.

Marciano, then 46 years old, was fitted with a toupee and ordered into training to lose 40 pounds so that he would more

Former Heavyweight Champion Joe Frazier

There is no love lost between Joe Frazier and Muhammad Ali, at least on Frazier's part. Frazier, the 1964 Olympic heavyweight gold medalist, felt that holding the world pro heavyweight championship from 1970 through 1973 should have been his glory days. After all, he had a professional record—32 wins, 4 losses, and 1 draw, with 27 technical knockouts—that deserved respect, if not adulation. When Ali set a title fight with Frazier as his comeback goal, however, taunts and derisions from the boisterous Louisville Lip bristled the less erudite son of a South Carolina sharecropper. Ali's words, "ignorant," "Uncle Tom," and "gorilla," cut deep.

Those words inflamed the public against Frazier so much that guards were needed to protect his children from threats of harm. Frazier wanted to pound those words back into Ali's lips. Despite his anger toward his opponent's behavior, however, the Southern country boy had a soft spot for the downtrodden. "Decent? I was more than decent," he said to Stephen Brunt for the book *Facing Ali: 15 Fighters, 15 Stories*. "I'm the man that's responsible for him getting his licen[s]e back. There's no doubt about that. And he knows that. I rode to New York and loaned him some money. I wasn't scared of him. Scared of who? He's got two legs like me. Two hands. A little more lips. I wasn't afraid of the guy. Anything I had to do to get him in those four squares, I would have done it within reason." Frazier lobbied within the boxing community and all the way to the president of the United States for Ali's return to the big arena.

closely resemble the fighter he had been in his prime. Day after day, the two fighters pulled punches and faked grunts and groans. Seven different endings to the fight were filmed—some showing wins for Marciano, some for Ali. The version that appeared on television and was advertised as being the computer's selection portrayed Marciano as the victor.

Ali was paid $999.99 for this work. He needed the money, and although he was game about his participation in this staged fight, it was the low point of his professional life.

GETTING BACK ON TRACK

By 1970, the war in Vietnam was dragging on, month after month, seemingly without end. Americans were growing impatient for a conclusion to the war—any conclusion—just so long as it allowed the United States to extricate itself honorably from a conflict that seemed to be unwinnable. Arum sensed that the Supreme Court would be more receptive to Ali's plea than they had been in 1967 or 1968. The legal team began to prepare Ali's case once more.

While one team was scheming for Ali in the halls of justice, Muhammad and his associates were plotting a comeback for Ali in the ring. Frazier, the reigning heavyweight champion, seemed to be the logical opponent for Ali, and both Frazier and his manager, Yank Durham, were keen for a match. The potential gate for such a fight was huge; it could gross as much as $40 million.

Governor Claude Kirk of Florida was the first politician to break the boycott imposed against Ali. Kirk announced that he would sanction an Ali fight in Tampa, Florida, but he was forced to retract his offer after there was tremendous political pressure not to support the fight. Other near misses at the beginning of Ali's comeback trail occurred in 1969 and 1970. Judge Roy Hofheinz, owner of the Houston Astrodome, lobbied in vain to stage the fight in his hometown. Ali soon received a boxing permit from John Bell Williams, the governor

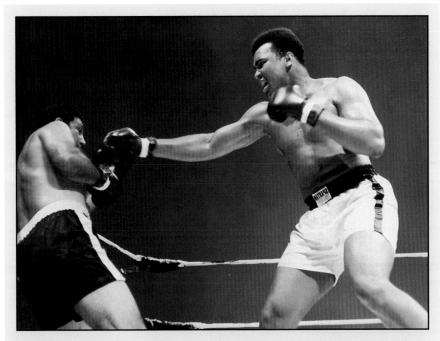

Because of the draft evasion charges against him, Ali was banned from boxing in the United States from 1967 to 1971. As new faces like Joe Frazier and George Foreman climbed to the top of the boxing world, Ali was forced to remain inactive or hold matches abroad. The only match Ali was allowed to participate in was a staged fight in 1970, seen here, with former heavyweight champion Rocky Marciano.

of Mississippi (normally a conservative politician in an ultra-conservative state), for an Ali–Frazier match in Jackson. As in Florida, the Mississippi deal fell through when news of it was leaked to the public.

In spite of these setbacks, the industrious Muhammad would not give up. He eventually reached an agreement with promoters to stage the fight in Toronto, Canada. Ali, whose passport had been revoked when he was convicted, could not win permission from the Supreme Court to leave the country for the 18 hours he would need in order to participate in the fight. An agreement that Muhammad reached with a Japanese promoter to hold the Frazier–Ali fight in Tokyo also had to be voided because of Ali's continuing passport problems.

Yet the momentum was building to let Ali practice his profession. On June 20, 1970, a court order overturned his suspension from boxing. Three months later, a deal was put together that would end his exile. Several powerful black politicians in Atlanta, Georgia, persuaded Mayor Sam Massell to grant Ali a license to fight there. These politicians exercised enough clout in Atlanta, which had a large black population, to secure a binding agreement; even the avowedly racist governor Lester Maddox did not move to block Ali's comeback. The date for the heavyweight championship fight was set for October 26, 1970.

At the last minute, Frazier's advisers, who had seemed so willing to have him fight Ali, backed down. They claimed that a prior binding agreement with another, less talented fighter prevented them from signing with Ali for the Atlanta fight. In fact, they were actually afraid that their man was not ready for Ali even though he had not fought professionally for more than three years.

Ali and the Atlanta promoters quickly found another major contender for him to fight: heavyweight Jerry Quarry. Without Frazier in the ring, the Atlanta match could not be considered a championship fight. Furthermore, the Supreme Court still had not rendered its final decision on Ali's appeal. Nevertheless, the bout against Quarry meant for the undefeated heavyweight that his exile would finally be over.

7

Resurrection of a Heavyweight

Ali's return to the ring in 1970 carried great symbolic importance to many people. During the 10 years that he had been a professional fighter, he had undergone several difficult personal ordeals and had witnessed many changes in relations between blacks and whites. Such circumstances had turned him into something of a mythical figure to his "people"; many blacks and other supporters had come to see him as a hero. Accordingly, they were hoping for him to achieve a victory against Quarry with an almost religious zeal.

To test the goodwill of the Georgia politicians, Ali held an exhibition match on September 2, 1970, several weeks after signing for the Quarry fight. The exhibition consisted of a series of one-round matches against a succession of lesser-ranked professional heavyweights and was held at Atlanta's Morehouse College gymnasium, which was designed to hold approximately 2,000. The gym was crammed with as many as

5,000 people on the day of the exhibition. When Ali was announced, the crowd—a widely diverse group of blacks and whites, laborers and college students, businessmen and hippies, the middle class and the urban poor—gave him a tumultuous welcome. The cheering began to ebb after a few rounds as Ali began to tire and show the effects of a three-year layoff.

Ali held off his opponents with precise technical boxing, but he did not dazzle the crowd with the emotional performance that they had come to see. His body hurt from the hits he took, his muscles ached, and his legs grew weak. By the fourth round, a few boos began to be heard among the crowd, which was becoming restless.

Drew "Bundini" Brown, Ali's confidant and assistant-trainer, talked to him at the end of the fourth round. As a leading member of Ali's entourage, he sensed the importance of this exhibition, Ali's first appearance after his exile. He exhorted the tired fighter, "This ain't no goddamn exhibition. This the Resurrection. These people out there, they bringin' you to life . . . they come to dig you out of the grave. . . . Tired? . . . Not now, champ. Straighten up."

Ali's reaction was one in which a person can actually see what a champion is made of. He took Bundini's words, which he knew to be true, and used them to fuel him through the last rounds of the exhibition. His weariness disappeared; he ignored his aches and pain. Filled with pride and desire, he rang in a handful of scintillating rounds as he danced and shuffled and popped shots off the heads of his opponents. The sound of his blows could be heard all the way to the farthest seats in the gym. His people responded with a howling, stomping, standing ovation.

In the five weeks between the exhibition match and the bout with Quarry, Ali trained hard at Angelo Dundee's Fifth Street Gym in Miami. He gradually regained his stamina, although he still was not at full strength by the time of the fight. Yet Ali's preparation went well—until the last day of training, when

Ali's suspension from boxing finally ended in 1970 when he was granted a license in Georgia and scheduled a match against heavyweight Jerry Quarry. Ali knocked out Quarry in his thirtieth straight professional victory.

a sparring partner named Blue Lewis landed a hard punch to his ribs. The blow shook Ali, and the round ended with him sagging to the mat. Dundee quickly hustled the spectators out of the gym.

NOT LOSING SIGHT OF THE PRIZE

That night, Ali was taken to a Cuban doctor who was a friend of Ali's ringside physician, Ferdie Pacheco. The doctor, who was trusted to keep the results of his examination a secret, x-rayed Ali's ribs. The x-rays showed no broken bones, although the ribs were deeply bruised.

The next day, Ali received two packages from an anonymous sender shortly before he left Miami for the fight in Atlanta. A note on one of the packages said only: "To Cassius Clay from Georgia." In one package was a dead black Chihuahua. In the other package was found a handmade doll that somewhat resembled Ali. A note next to the doll read: "We know how to handle black draft-dodging dogs in Georgia. Stay out of Atlanta." Ali buried the little dog; he kept the doll. It would inspire him to get ready for the fight.

Even though Ali's ribs were causing him much pain, he knew that he could not postpone the Quarry fight. To do so would risk the gains he had made thus far. Besides, even at half strength and with bruised ribs, he was confident that he could beat Quarry. He had fought Liston in their second fight with bruised ribs, although he had been lucky that the Liston rematch had lasted only one round. Still, Quarry was not in the same class as Liston.

Even if Ali was somewhat less than fully ready for Quarry, the public—as had been demonstrated at the exhibition—was ready for Ali. By the day of the fight, October 26, 1970, Atlanta's hotels were filled with a wide range of people—including many celebrities—who had come to the city to attend the fight. By the time of the match, the atmosphere surrounding the event resembled a convention for people whose dress and demeanor were extravagant and often outrageous: Men wore mink porkpie hats, tuxedos, and full-length fur coats; women had on diamonds and bright, glittery evening gowns.

The two boxers entered the arena. The referee read the rules to them; the boxers touched gloves with each other and returned to their corners. Then the bell rang, and the crowd was on its feet and yelling. Ali was finally back.

Quarry tried to take the fight to Ali in the first round. He came in close to Ali in an attempt to slug it out with the former champion. Ali was ready for this tactic. Whenever Quarry charged him, he spun away from the approaching fighter and danced to the left, but not before landing a jab or a combination of hooks and jabs. The crowd was pleased. This was the familiar, dancing Ali, frustrating his opponent with his quick feet and hurting him with his fast hands.

Ali moved faster in the first round than he had in any fight since the Liston matches. It was quite a show by the 28-year-old grand master of boxing, and at the bell the crowd stood on its feet again to applaud him. The second round went much the same as the first: Quarry rushed Ali, who skipped around the ring and hit Quarry with a few lightning-quick combinations before retreating. By the end of the first two rounds, Quarry had hardly touched Ali.

Quarry slowed down a little in the third round, and in response, so did Ali. Still dancing, but attacking rather than retreating, he hit Quarry with some hard shots. Suddenly, a little over halfway through the round, he hit Quarry with a left hook that opened up a gash over Quarry's left eye. With the blood from the cut impairing Quarry's vision, Ali began to hit the wounded fighter with a furious volley of punches, pummeling him until the bell sounded the end of the third round.

Quarry's manager, seeing that the cut over his fighter's eye was too deep to patch up adequately, threw in the towel before the start of the fourth round, and the fight was stopped. Ali had won his thirtieth professional fight without a loss, and Quarry had been his twenty-fourth knockout victim.

Sportswriter Steve Cady of the *New York Times* hailed Ali as a "black prince, a folk hero who convinced white America that blacks really existed." Ali himself picked up this black–white theme in a later interview in which he expressed his emotions about the fight. He said, "When I climb into the ring, I'm thinking about God, and I'm thinking about all those people in every ghetto in every city in the United States of America. I'm out to whip all the hypocrites of the power structure. I'm fighting for my freedom and carrying the hopes of my 30 million black people here."

Ali, hero or devil incarnate (depending on one's way of seeing things), was most definitely back in full form. Ali later called himself, "three and a half years out of shape" in the best selling book *Muhammad Ali: His Life and Times*. It would be only a matter of time before Frazier was forced to take his measure. Ali had to fight only one more contender, the South American Oscar Bonavena, before Frazier finally agreed to confront him.

BATTLE ROYAL—ALI VS. FRAZIER

Shortly after Ali dispatched Bonavena with a knockout in the fifteenth round, he and Frazier set March 8, 1971, as the date for their historic showdown. The site was Ali's favorite haunt from earlier days, Madison Square Garden in New York City. Warming to his latest opponent, Ali predicted a sixth-round knockout of Frazier.

The fight is still regarded as one of the classic contests in boxing history. In many ways, it led to a new era in boxing. For the first time in history, a championship fight was viewed by a truly worldwide audience. Approximately 300 million people watched the match on closed-circuit television. Madison Square Garden broke all of its records by selling an amazing $1,350,000 worth of tickets for the privilege of viewing the fight live in the arena.

Frazier and his manager, Yank Durham, were as savvy a pair of strategists as existed in boxing. Yet their plan to beat Ali was brutally simple: Kill the body and the head will follow. This meant that Frazier was to pound Ali's stomach, ribs, chest, and back relentlessly—until Ali was in such pain that he would lose his concentration. Then Frazier would go for the knockout punch to the head.

The trouble with this strategy—as Durham and Frazier knew—was that many other boxers had tried to catch Ali before but none had succeeded. No one had ever come close to seriously hurting him. Frazier had proved that he could punch and that he could take a punch. He was built solidly, yet he was surprisingly quick for his size.

The fight began predictably enough. Like Quarry and many others, Frazier came right at Ali. What Ali did was astonishing. Rather than dancing to avoid Frazier's rush, he positioned himself on the ropes, leaning into them and then bouncing off them, and fought Frazier straight on. Ali later nicknamed this tactic "rope-a-dope" to indicate that the opponent who had resolved to pound Ali's body while he protected himself on the ropes was a fool: Such an opponent would wear himself out by punching Ali's arms, gloves, and elbows; he would then be vulnerable to a comparatively fresher Ali several rounds later. Ali's presumption was that his opponent would eventually tire, at which point he could counterattack and try for a knockout.

Frazier's big punch—his knockout blow—was his left hook, which Ali avoided mainly by using his own left as the lead

Former Heavyweight Champion Joe Frazier

"He was Goliath, I was David. And I had a repeat slingshot," Joe Frazier said laughingly to Stephen Brunt for his *Facing Ali* book. "My slingshot just kept coming back over and over, you know what I mean? Not just in the fifteenth round. . . . Every round. *Every* round. This guy got hurt every round. Look at the fight." Frazier was talking about the first professional defeat delivered to Ali.

"It was great. My dream came true. And I lived up to my word. I said I was going to help him get a licen[s]e, and then I was going to dust him off. I used to sit back and watch him on television. I said, 'Lord, I'm going next week or next month against this man. I'm not asking for something unworthy. I want you to help me kill the scamboogah.' That's what I said to the Lord. I said, 'This guy ain't right. This guy just ain't right.' Anything that he ever done, it seemed like it was so glorious or so great. What has *the* greatest ever done that's so great? I want everybody to sit back and look at it. What have he done so great for this world? Everything that he has done was against this country. When are we going to open our eyes up and see? When are we going to start seeing? You all ask the Lord. Don't ask me."

punch. If a fighter's lead punch against a left-handed opponent is a right, then he puts himself in a dangerous position when his lead misses: His right hand and arm are fully extended, so he cannot protect himself from an oncoming punch when his opponent strikes back with a left. It is basic boxing strategy to lead with the left against a left-handed boxer, and Ali followed this strategy to perfection.

By the third round, Frazier had thrown an awful lot of punches at Ali's body, most of which Ali had deflected or had been absorbed by his arms, elbows, or gloves. Ali then chose to stop bouncing off the ropes; he stood flat-footed and traded swings with Frazier. When he backed Frazier across the ring, he spoke to the fighter. He told Frazier that he had not been hurt by him and then taunted Frazier to come at him.

Their vicious toe-to-toe fighting continued in the fourth round, when Frazier hit Ali with a clean shot to the head that drew first blood. Frazier soon began to dominate. He hit Ali's body and then caught him with a couple of straight jabs to the head.

By the fifth round, it was Frazier's turn to taunt Ali. He held his hands low and let Ali take shots at him, many of which missed. At the end of the round, he derided Ali by patting him on the top of his head. The rhythm of the fight flattened out in the sixth, seventh, and eighth rounds. Frazier continued to work on Ali's body with thunderous hooks to the ribs, and the two fighters traded occasional jabs to the head. In the ninth round, the tempo of the fight changed dramatically when Ali stunned Frazier with a hook. Ali was suddenly all over Frazier, who wobbled around the ring and covered up his face with his gloves. The triumph of Ali's rope-a-dope tactics appeared imminent, but he could not put Frazier away.

When the bell rang, Frazier stumbled to his corner. He was given smelling salts to clear his head, and water was toweled over his body to refresh him. Ali would later regret not finishing off Frazier in the ninth round.

In the tenth round, Ali was too tired from his exertion in the previous round, and Frazier was too cautious and stunned to repeat another direct confrontation. While both fighters threw an occasional leaden punch, this and the next round provided time for them to gather their strength.

Frazier, who was visibly worn out but showed tremendous heart, came back strong in the twelfth round. He launched an all-out attack on Ali, hitting him with right-jab–left-hook combinations that shook him but did not knock him out. These blows marked the last burst of energy from either fighter. During the next two rounds, they seemed to waltz around the ring, hanging on to each other like drunken dinosaurs.

Just when it appeared as though the fight would end without a climax, a wild left hook—Frazier's best punch—near the end of the fifteenth and final round sent Ali thudding to the canvas. Frazier stared in disbelief as Ali tried to pick himself off the mat. The referee moved in to give Ali a count. The crowd began to roar.

Ali made it to his feet, and for a moment both fighters just stared at each other. Seconds later, the fight was over. Ali and Frazier went to their respective corners and collapsed on their stools, waiting as the judges huddled together to total their scores for the fight. A microphone was eventually placed before the ring announcer, who said in time-honored fashion, "Ladies and gentlemen . . ." and proceeded to read out the points given by the judges before announcing their decision, " . . . and still the champion, Joe Frazier."

It had been, according to the *Times*, a "monumental epic fight." Yet it was also Ali's first loss in a professional fight. Frazier was still the champion.

The fight was a stunning reversal for Ali. Suddenly, he seemed human again. He was not invincible; he could be beaten by a tough and determined fighter. Nevertheless, it had taken a superhuman effort by Frazier for him to win. Ali was still a major contender—perhaps *the* major contender—for the championship. Knowing this, Frazier and his advisers would avoid scheduling a rematch with Ali for as long as they could.

COMEBACK TRAIL

Three and a half months after Ali lost the title bout, he won his political freedom. On June 28, 1971, the Supreme Court ruled unanimously that his conviction was invalid. In light of the conclusion by the selective service hearing officer—the only individual to carefully examine the petitioner and other witnesses in person—that the defendant qualified as a conscientious objector and no grounds to the contrary were offered by the Selective Service Board at the time of its rejection, the Supreme Court reversed the decision of the lower court. In Justice William O. Douglas's opinion, "What Clay's testimony adds up to is that he believes only in war as sanctioned by the Koran, that is to say, a religious war against nonbelievers. All other wars are unjust." He was subsequently granted the status of conscientious objector to the military draft on the grounds of his religious beliefs.

The Supreme Court vindicated Ali by ruling against the government on three points. First, the court found that Ali's objection to serving in the armed forces was based on religious

IN HIS OWN WORDS...

Ali recalled for his biography by author Thomas Hauser:

> The whole time I wasn't allowed to fight, no matter what the authorities said, it felt like I was the heavyweight champion of the world. . . . Then I lost to Joe Frazier. And what hurt most wasn't the money that losing cost me. It wasn't the punches I took. It was knowing that my title was gone. When I beat Sonny Liston, I was too young to appreciate what I'd won. But when I lost to Frazier, I would have done anything except go against the will of Allah to get my title back again.

training and belief. (The government had claimed that Ali's desire to avoid the draft was not based on religious grounds.) Second, the court rejected the government's claim that Ali was not sincere in his beliefs. Third, the court dismissed as irrelevant the government's claim that Ali was not opposed to all wars. The court found that the last point had not been an issue in the government's case during the first appeal in New Orleans and thus, by procedure and tradition, should not be considered by the U.S. Supreme Court, either.

Another less publicized victory was achieved that year. President Lyndon B. Johnson had charged the Selective Service to work with state governors to establish greater diversity in its system. In 1971 his request became a legal provision that local membership be judiciously representative of the racial and national origin of registrants in the area served by the board.

With the issue of his draft status resolved once and for all, Ali could devote his full attention to regaining the heavyweight title. In a sense, he was in the same position after the Frazier fight as he had been before he was able to fight for the title against Liston in 1964: He had to prove himself by methodically fighting his way to another championship match. There was one main difference between his path to the title in 1964 and the one he had to take in 1971. In 1964, Liston had taken Ali too lightly and had paid the price. The second time around, the handful of top contenders knew how good Ali was and tried to avoid him.

Ali took part in three more fights in 1971 and in six fights in 1972. He won all of them, including six by knockout. On January 22, 1973, Frazier was dethroned by former Olympic gold medalist George Foreman. To Frazier, the loss of the title meant that he might be more willing to fight Ali.

Ali proceeded with his climb back to the top of the boxing world by fighting a little-known boxer named Ken Norton in San Diego, California, in March 1973. Ali did not take Norton as seriously as he should have. He also had some especially bad

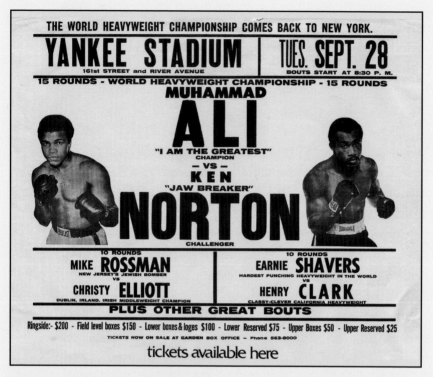

Little-known fighter Ken Norton dealt Ali his second professional loss in March 1973, but in their September rematch Ali redeemed himself by winning, despite having a broken hand. Ali's win in the bout, advertised by this flier, set up his rematch with Joe Frazier, and his battle with George Foreman the next year.

luck on the night of the fight, which took place in Norton's home state.

Norton swung wildly and not very expertly throughout the entire fight. In the first round, he landed what Ali felt was a lucky punch to the side of his face. The punch broke Ali's jaw. Not wanting to give his opponent a psychological lift, Ali did not show any reaction, even though he was in terrible pain.

The pain caused Ali to lose his concentration, and he was not very sharp. Norton beat him to the punch during most of the fight. Ali never mounted an effective counterattack to

Norton's aggressive style, although he managed to last through all 12 rounds of the fight. The judges ruled in favor of Norton, the local favorite. The fight, which was Ali's second professional loss, caused many commentators to agree with sportswriter William Wallace's assessment in the *Times* that "it was all very sad the beginning of the end of the line" for Ali. Ali, however, would not allow himself to be put into retirement so easily. He immediately booked a rematch with Norton for the following September in Los Angeles. Yet he continued to be jinxed by Norton. In the sixth round, he broke a bone in his hand while hitting Norton, and he had to fight mostly one-handed for the remainder of the bout. Still, Ali beat Norton by putting on a smart, classic boxing exhibition that confused his opponent and clearly demonstrated Ali's superiority as a fighter.

By beating Norton, Ali set himself up for his second major fight since the end of his exile. He signed with Frazier for a rematch, to be held again at Madison Square Garden, on January 28, 1974. It was understood that the winner of this match would then meet Foreman for the heavyweight championship.

ALI-FRAZIER REVISITED

Ali was eager for a second fight with Frazier. "I think we should do it again," he said, "because we draw more people to an event than anybody in the recorded history of records." His estimation was not far off. While he would not clear the $2.5 million he made from his first fight with Frazier, he did receive $1.7 million for the fight, which was billed as Ali–Frazier II. It was his largest payday in almost three years.

The first Ali–Frazier fight had gone 15 rounds; their rematch was scheduled for a merciful 12 rounds. Ali had learned a few things about Frazier during their first fight—the most important point being that he would get nowhere playing rope-a-dope with the roughhousing Philadelphian. Instead, he chose to box Frazier.

During their rematch, Ali was seldom on the ropes. Instead, he danced a little and clinched a lot. Whenever the referee pried him away from Frazier, Ali jabbed him as he moved.

Ali almost won the fight near the end of the second round with a solid left hook that knocked Frazier to the floor. Unfortunately for Ali, someone yelled out, "Bell." This cry confused the referee, who stopped the fight for almost 20 seconds. The pause gave Frazier enough time to get off the canvas and clear his head, but the brief respite proved to be of little further help to Frazier. Ali eluded him for most of the fight, and the judges ultimately awarded the victory to Ali.

Sportswriter Red Smith reported that the two fighters "came in as former champions, both beaten, both past their prime." Smith was right only on one point—that they both had been beaten before. Ali was about to show the world that he was far from being a has-been. (For additional information on Ali's most famous opponents, enter "Joe Frazier," "George Foreman," or "Ken Norton" into any search engine and browse the sites listed.)

8

The Greatest

Ali's incessant desire to push himself further than he has ever been took him in 1974 to a large, modern structure built in a clearing in the jungle outside Kinshasa, Zaire, in Africa. The structure, known as 20th of May Stadium, had the look of an American football arena. Yet there was also something sinister about it.

For one thing, the stadium was already beginning to decay even though it was only a few years old. The ruin was subtle yet pervasive: Bits of concrete had fallen off the structure; weeds were growing at various places in the floor; cracks had appeared in some of the support columns. The stadium had been built quickly, shoddily, and expensively as a symbol of the potency of one of Africa's most long-lived and brutal dictatorships, the reign of Colonel Joseph Mobutu.

It was both proper and ironic that Ali's destiny led him to Zaire, on the continent of his ancestors. It was proper because he had always taken great pride in his African ancestry and encouraged other black Americans to do likewise. It was ironic because the reason for his visit to Zaire, which was to fight Foreman, proved to be one of the greatest promotional hypes in boxing history.

The Rumble in the Jungle, as the Ali–Foreman fight was dubbed, was the result of Mobutu's attempt to gain respectability for his country and an American boxing promoter's urge for a flamboyant and moneymaking promotion. Mobutu of Zaire and promoter Don King of Cleveland had little knowledge of one another before Ali's rematch with Frazier at Madison Square Garden. Following Ali's victory, however, the greed and vanity that eventually led to the slugfest at 20th of May Stadium were set in motion.

King was the one promoter who had the connections to put together an Ali–Foreman fight. Ali was ready to take on Foreman, but the champion and his managers were reluctant to meet Ali. When King found out through Muhammad that the nation of Zaire had offered money guarantees for as much as $5 million for each fighter, he knew he would be able to get Foreman to sign a contract for the fight.

Agents of the two fighters met with Zairian representatives until they finally reached an agreement. All sorts of organizations and individuals had staged and promoted fights in the 100 years since the advent of modern boxing, but Zaire became the first national government to accept these roles. The fight was to be held in early October 1974, and the two fighters were each guaranteed $5 million.

Ali faced an awesome, though not thoroughly tested, opponent in Foreman. He was big; at 220–225 pounds, he was bigger than Ali, bigger than Frazier, and even more of a bear than Liston, who had been one of Foreman's heroes. Like Liston, he enjoyed knocking out his opponents early. He had needed only a total of 11.5 minutes—less than four complete rounds—to dispatch Joe "King" Roman, Frazier, and Norton. Also like

Liston, Foreman was a hard puncher. His favorite punch was his "anywhere" punch, so named because "anywhere it hits you it breaks something inside you." This punch could be either a right or left hook—usually to the body. Either hook was devastating. The writer Norman Mailer, who covered the fight in Zaire, described Foreman's main weapon as a "a big hook, heavy as death, oppressive as the closing of one's tomb."

RUMBLE IN THE JUNGLE

Ali was not frightened by the prospect of going against such a hard-hitting young fighter. If anything, he relished the challenge. Even though critics had said that Ali was finished and that at 32 he was too old to fight, he knew he was not like other boxers. He had extraordinary intuitive skills that told him when to lay back and when to push ahead.

In addition, if Ali beat Foreman, he would become only the second man ever to win the heavyweight title twice. The other fighter to do this was Floyd Patterson. No one had ever won it three times. Because others said that Ali was too old to fight and because winning meant being the heavyweight champion once again, he drove himself relentlessly to prepare himself for the bout. He trained the entire summer before the match at his camp in the mountains of Pennsylvania, and he arrived in Zaire a month before the fight to acclimatize himself to the smothering African heat. He was looking forward to regaining the title that had been taken away from him in 1967, when he was at the peak of his career.

Foreman suffered a cut over his eye during a sparring session, and the fight had to be postponed for a few weeks. By the night of the fight, October 30, Ali was—both physically and psychologically—in the best shape since the end of his exile. The match was broadcast via satellite to closed-circuit television venues in America as well as to theaters and halls in many other countries of the world. To accommodate the American audience, the fight began in Zaire at an unusual hour: 2:00 A.M.

Despite suggestions by the media that Ali was a former champion past his prime, he continued to push himself physically and mentally. Here, Ali trains in Zaire for his 1974 "Rumble in the Jungle" against defending heavyweight champion George Foreman.

Fight spectators, as many as 80,000 of them, jammed into 20th of May Stadium. In the United States, the bout was viewed by millions more in sold-out theaters across the country. Former boxing champions Jack Dempsey and Gene Tunney were among the many who turned out to watch a less than perfect broadcast on a giant screen in Madison Square Garden, where the shifting images that appeared on the screen in front of them seemed as though they could have been filmed on the moon rather than in equatorial Africa.

To the cheers of "*Ali bomaye!*" (which roughly means "Kill him, Ali!"), the older fighter made his way down the aisle to the ring. He was dressed in natty white satin boxing trunks with black piping and a white silk African robe. Foreman entered next, wearing his characteristic patriotic colors: red velvet trunks with white stripes and a blue waistband. As the referee read the rules, Ali started to work on the psyche of Foreman, telling him, "You have heard of me since you were young. You've been following me since you were a little boy. Now you meet me, your master."

At the sound of the opening bell, the two fighters charged out of their corners, ran up to each other, and backed away as if repelled by magnetic force. They stalked each other around the ring, feeling each other out; then Ali got in the first two blows—hard rights to Foreman's head—before tying him up in a clinch to ward off a counterpunch. Foreman disengaged from Ali and, as he had been trained to do, followed Ali around the ring, lumbering after him like a rhinoceros, cutting him off at the corners so that he could not dance away. Once he had cut off Ali, he attacked with right and left haymakers to the body—anywhere punches. Ali felt them.

Ali realized quickly that Foreman was well trained in stopping his movement. He responded instinctively by moving to the ropes, where he covered himself as well as he could while Foreman unloaded his doomsday punches. Ali was playing rope-a-dope again—only this time, unlike the first Frazier fight, he was in perfect condition.

For some reason, the ropes had not been wound as tightly as they should have been. This gave Ali room in which to work. He often leaned far back into the ropes so that he could dodge or better absorb Foreman's blows. Nevertheless, he knew that playing rope-a-dope would put him in trouble if the fight went the full 15 rounds.

Ali followed his instinct to play rope-a-dope during the first three rounds even though Dundee was screaming at him from his corner to move, to dance. He also kept up the chatter directed at Foreman, telling him, among other things, "Shoot your best shot."

Foreman's best shots were almost enough to finish the fight. Several of them took Ali to the threshold of a place he has described as the "dream room." According to Ali, when a fighter receives a jolting blow, the door to the dream room "opens, and you see neon orange and green lights blinking. You see bats blowing trumpets; alligators play trombones; and snakes are screaming. Weird masks and actor's clothes hang on the wall." Because Ali had seen these things before, he did not panic. He shot a few right jabs—leads—off Foreman's head; he surprised Foreman with these right leads because they exposed his body and thus go against the norm of boxing.

In the fourth and fifth rounds, Foreman began to tire in the sultry African heat, and Ali rose to the attack. He popped off the ropes more often, hitting Foreman with smart combinations that snapped his head around. As Ali began to move, Foreman followed, but he was no longer the determined rhinoceros of the early rounds. Instead, he plodded after Ali. He had clearly grown leg weary.

By the seventh round, Ali began to dominate the fight, striking Foreman with a number of quick jabs. His body hurt from Foreman's earlier punches and he knew that Foreman's second wind might come soon, however, so Ali stayed off the ropes and began to press the attack in the eighth round.

Just before the bell, Ali hit Foreman with a right–left–right combination that staggered the younger fighter. He tiptoed to the ropes, doubtlessly seeing the laughing lizards and bats playing saxophone for the first time in his career. Pinned against the ropes, as Ali had been in the first rounds, Foreman was hit with the coup de grace: three big rights that sent him on a slow-motion odyssey around the ring one last time, until he collapsed slowly; it took a full 20 seconds for him to fall into a heap in the center of the canvas.

Not one single person in the stadium remained in his seat. On the large screen in Madison Square Garden, the voices of the announcers were drowned out by the cheers. In the flickering

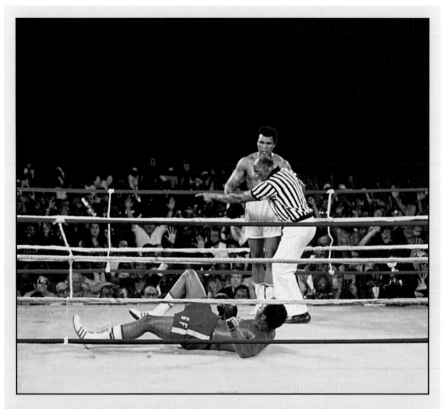

Ali is restrained by a referee after knocking out defending champion George Foreman and regaining the heavyweight title. The title match, broadcast around the world, produced millions in revenue and solidified Ali's status as "the Greatest."

light of the arena, the New York crowd heard only two words being chanted over and over again: "*Ali bomaye!*"

In his dressing room after the fight, a jubilant Ali said, "I told you he was nothing, but did you listen. . . . I told you I was the greatest of all time. Never again say I'm the underdog until I'm 50 years of age."

This last statement by Ali was classic playacting. He had quietly announced before the bout that he was considering retirement after the Foreman fight, win or lose. It was the first time that he had ever mentioned retirement.

In the flush of victory after the match, Ali decided to keep on fighting. He would ring in a few more bouts and enjoy some large paydays. After all, he was the champion once again; he might as well enjoy the privileges that came with being at the top.

Ali figured that he could quit whenever he wanted to. Yet he would find that it would be harder to do so than to become champion. The lure of the limelight and the big sums of money he was making would keep him fighting for longer than was good for him. For the time being, who could argue with his decision to continue fighting? He had triumphed over his opponents, over the U.S. government, over age, seemingly over mortality itself. He was, as he himself said, the Greatest.

The Foreman fight was Ali's last bout in 1974. The following year, he fought four times. Three of these fights were against much lesser opponents; the last fight was against Frazier. Ali never made less than $1 million for each of these bouts. For the Frazier fight, held in the Philippines, he earned $4 million.

Ali began to train less often after the Foreman fight. Training was the toughest part of boxing as well as the least glamorous. The routine was indispensable for preparing a fighter's body and mind for the sport.

Ali did not even bother to spar for the Frazier fight. Instead, he began to indulge himself in the high life with the money he was making. He ate well and put on weight. Although he usually took most of it off before a match, he never regained the conditioning he had achieved for the Foreman fight.

Ali also began to see women other than his second wife, Belinda. By the time he established a training camp in Manila in the Philippines for the Frazier fight, he and Belinda were close to a divorce. Ali introduced his companion of the moment, Veronica Porche, as his wife to the president of the Philippines, Ferdinand Marcos. This gaffe was picked up by the U.S. newspapers the week before the fight. Ali reacted angrily to the news coverage of his private life, saying, "This is going too far. They got me for the draft. They got me for my religion. They got me for all sorts of things. But they shouldn't be able to get me for my girlfriend."

THRILLA IN MANILA

The third Ali–Frazier bout, known as the Thrilla in Manila, was held on October 1, 1975. Ali's last truly great fight, the match was a wild, seesaw affair, with first one man taking control, then the other. In this respect, it was much like the other two fights between them.

Perhaps because Ali was not in the best of shape, it was he—and not Frazier—who came out quickly, looking for the early knockout. Ali dominated the first rounds, but Frazier, as always, was doggedly determined to win and turned the contest into a ferocious fight. By the fourteenth round, Frazier's face resembled a lumpy peach. His eyes were almost swollen shut, and he could scarcely walk. His trainer, Eddie Futch, stopped the fight by not letting his man come out for the bell in the fifteenth round.

When it was all over, Ali knew that he had fought his toughest fight. Although he had won, he may have damaged himself in the process. After the fight, he commented, "You may have seen the last of Ali. I want to get out. I'm tired and on top. What you saw tonight was next to death. [Frazier] he's the toughest man in the world."

After Ali's courageous performance, Red Smith, who had not always been a fan of Ali's, wrote in the *Times*:

> Say what you will about this noisy extrovert, this swaggering, preening, play-acting slice of theatrical ham: the man is a gladiator. He was a callow braggart of 22 when Sonny Liston surrendered the title to him 11 years ago. At the ripe age of 33 he is a champion of genuine quality.

Ali's third fight with Joe Frazier, nicknamed the "Thrilla in Manila," took place on October 1, 1975 in Manila, Philippines. In his last great bout, Ali defeated Frazier to retain his heavyweight title. Here, he celebrates with President Ferdinand Marcos of the Philippines, promoter Don King, brother Rahman, and father Cassius Marcellus Clay Sr.

WANING FIGHTER

Ali did not fight again for almost a whole year. When he finally came back to the ring, he made it worth his while. The fight was against Norton—their third match. It was held at Yankee Stadium in New York on a cool night on September 28, 1976. Ali was guaranteed a record $6 million for the bout. The live gate brought in $3.5 million, breaking the longstanding record of $2.6 million established by the Jack Dempsey–Gene Tunney fight held at Soldier Field in Chicago almost a half century earlier.

Ali was cocky as usual before the fight. Even though he was in awful shape, he predicted a knockout in five rounds. The fight went the full 15 rounds again, and throughout the fight, Ali never threw a punch that hurt Norton. He outboxed Ali in most of the rounds.

At the end of the match, the judges awarded the victory to Ali—reigning champions are rarely voted against in a fight that goes the distance. James J. Braddock had been the last reigning heavyweight champion deposed by the judges' verdict. That had taken place 41 years before, in a fight against Max Schmeling. Before Braddock, only two other heavyweight champions had lost a verdict: Schmeling to Dempsey in 1932 and Dempsey to Tunney in 1926.

Ali accepted the decision and the money, but uncharacteristically, he had little to say after the fight. Several days later, on a visit to Turkey with Wallace Muhammad, the eldest son of Elijah Muhammad, who had become the new leader of the Nation of Islam after his father's death, Ali announced his retirement from boxing. He was going to dedicate himself to the Islamic cause. Whether or not he stayed out of the ring for good would depend on how much money he was offered to fight again and, perhaps even more importantly, the requirements of his ego.

9

The Champion of Change

Ali made a sincere effort to devote his life exclusively to Islam. Spurred on by Wallace Muhammad's challenge that he "use his power—the fist of his tongue, instead of the fist of the ring—for truth," he traveled all over to talk about his experiences since his conversion to Islam. The thrill of public adulation, once experienced in the ring, was hard to leave behind, though, and the money was still there, waiting to be picked up at the stroke of a pen; all Ali had to do was sign a contract to fight. He was away from the ring for only seven months.

Ali's first fight after his retirement took place on May 16, 1977, in Landover, Maryland, against Alfredo Evangelista. When another heavyweight champion, Joe Louis, had run out of worthy opponents in the late 1930s, he began to fight what the press labeled "a bum a month." Evangelista was the sort of fighter who, had he practiced his trade in Louis's day, probably would have been put into that same category.

Although Ali had retired from the ring, he had never taken the final steps that were required of him to renounce his championship; also, less than a year had passed since his last title defense. Because of these two facts, he was still considered to be the undisputed heavyweight champion—and as the champion, he was able to command a lordly $2.5 million guarantee for the Evangelista match. Ali's choice of Evangelista, who was not a top contender, as his next opponent indicated that the current heavyweight champion might have learned from Louis how to pick up some easy money.

Ali began training for Evangelista about eight weeks before the fight. When the champion set up training camp, he weighed in at a bloated 240 pounds. He managed to slim down to a respectable 221 pounds by the day of the official fight weigh-in.

Ali in his prime would have taken four or five rounds to destroy Evangelista, but at the age of 35, he was not able to finish off his opponent. The fight went the full fifteen rounds. Ali was not sharp; he moved ponderously around the ring. He clinched and covered up well, and he managed to keep Evangelista at a distance during most of the fight, but his punches had little power.

In spite of Ali's pitiful performance, he won the fight on the judges' decision—the tradition that a reigning heavyweight champion does not lose a fight on points held up. Sportswriter Randy Neumann noted in the *Times*:

> Ali, being a living legend, is a hometown fighter wherever he fights. The world is his backyard. Only he can score points lying on the ropes, dancing around. . . . Beating Ali by decision is like giving Jack Nicklaus a stroke a hole. You're beat before you start.

FACING YOUNGER CHALLENGERS

An unusual and disturbing pattern in Ali's fights was becoming evident. As he grew older, he was having to fight longer. He had not been able to win any of his last six fights—including the Evangelista bout—before the eleventh round. Ali's doctor, Ferdie Pacheco, noted after the champion faced Evangelista, "Ali is now at the dangerous mental point where his heart and mind are no longer in it.... It's just a payday. It's almost as if an actor played his role too long. He's just mouthing the words."

Ignoring his poor showing and the danger to his health that had been alluded to by Pacheco, Ali continued his routine of picking up a few million dollars every eight months or so. He also found some new ways to keep himself in the public eye. In 1977, he starred in *The Greatest*, the film version of his autobiography. The following year, he lent his name and voice to "Muhammad Ali," a television cartoon series for children.

On February 15, 1978, Ali fought another so-called bum of the month, the largely unknown Leon Spinks. More than 10 years younger than the 36-year-old Ali, he was a former marine from St. Louis, Missouri, with only seven professional fights to his credit. Although he possessed a wild, awkward boxing style, he was hungry for the crown. "I'm a pecking chicken," he told reporters, "and Ali's got the gold I really want."

To many sportswriters, Spinks, who had fought such nonentities as "Lightning" Bob Smith and Scott LeDoux, seemed destined for oblivion rather than for the heavyweight crown. To these writers, his toughest fight seemed to have been the one he once had with his brother Michael, who was also a fighter, over a baloney sandwich. Accordingly, an Ali–Spinks fight seemed like more than a little baloney, too.

Ali's fight against Spinks also went the full fifteen rounds. Spinks—unlike Evangelista or Norton—was all over Ali throughout the fight, trapping him in the corners and pounding him, breaking through his peak-a-boo crouch. Ali tried to dance, but his feet would not respond. Instead, he dragged himself around the ring.

At the end of the fight, boxing tradition was shattered. For the first time in 43 years, a reigning champion lost a judges'

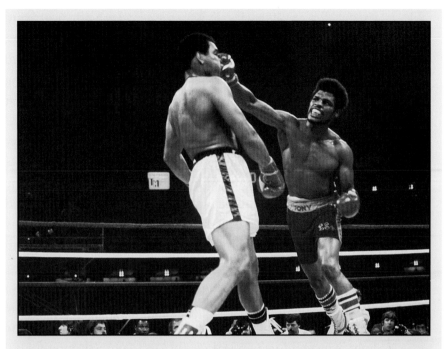

Ali was shaken by his loss to unknown heavyweight Leon Spinks in their first meeting in 1978. He trained intensely for their rematch later that year and defeated Spinks to become heavyweight champion for a record third time.

decision. Spinks became the new heavyweight champion of the world.

TIME TO GET TOUGH

The loss to Spinks seemed to awaken Ali. He demanded and received a rematch with the young champion, which was set for September 15, 1978, in New Orleans. To get back in shape, Ali set a grueling training regimen for himself. He rented a secluded bungalow on Lake Pontchartrain in Louisiana in late July and ran three to five miles every day. He worked on strengthening his torso by doing 12 different kinds of sit-ups; one of his assistant trainers estimated he did 8,000 sit-ups in the month and a half that preceded the fight. He also set up a special diet for himself. He began every day with two trout, eggs, and unbuttered toast; he then washed down salt, iron, and potassium tablets with a glass of orange juice. He also had an emotional and psychological advantage to help him along with his training: If he beat Spinks, he would become the first heavyweight ever to win the title three times.

While Ali was rebuilding, Spinks was busy at work destroying himself. Spinks's hangers-on had persuaded him to fire George Benton, the manager who had helped him become the champion. Sam Solomon, one of Spinks's buddies, replaced Benton. Solomon did not have a plan for Spinks to follow when fighting Ali. Solomon was also very lax when it came to handling the fantastically undisciplined young boxer.

Two weeks before the fight was to take place, Spinks's brother Michael called Benton back in to help; it had become obvious that the young champion was unprepared for the fight. The call for help was already too late; Solomon would not give up his job. Consequently, Benton and Solomon worked out a ludicrous deal that split the management of Spinks's fight between them: They would trade the duty of managing Spinks during every other round of the fight.

"I've said this many times before about Ali," Benton warned about the fighter's combination of luck, skill, and determination. "Liston. Foreman. Frazier. The draft thing. Ali always comes up on his feet. It's like there's some mystical force guiding his life, making him not like other men. When I think of that . . . it's scary."

Seven days before the fight, Spinks disappeared into the seedy bars of New Orleans. He was finally found several days later and was brought back to his camp to sober up. The night before the fight, he stayed up until the wee hours of the morning, drinking with his friends and some women who had attached themselves to his camp.

The final act of unprofessionalism in the Spinks camp occurred just before the bout. While dressing for the fight in the locker room, Spinks discovered that his entourage had forgotten to bring his protective cup, water bucket, and water bottles. He had to borrow this equipment from another fighter.

Ali came out in the first round determined to give Spinks a boxing lesson. The veteran fought an elegant fight—not overpowering (he was too old to manage that) but stylish. He circled left and jabbed repeatedly, hitting Spinks's head as though it were a speed bag. When Ali, who outweighed Spinks by 20 pounds, became the target of a Spinks charge, he rudely grabbed the younger man, held him in a clinch for a while, then pushed him away so that he could jab him some more.

By the fifth round, Ali was stinging Spinks with a combination of punches, and Spinks was openly looking to his corner for advice, Benton, who had become fed up with the alternating-round system of managing, had left the auditorium during that round, not to return. Although the fight went the full fifteen rounds, no one was surprised when the ringside announcer intoned after it was over that the new heavyweight champion of the world was Ali. An impressed Spinks said after the fight, "He was always my idol. He still is."

Having won the heavyweight championship for a third time, Ali was now ready to retire. The physical ordeal of boxing was becoming too much for him, and now that he was older, the glitter of stardom finally seemed less important to him than it had once been. He said:

> God, I have suffered and suffered and suffered. It really hurts. It's time for a new life. . . . I don't want to fight no more. I've been doing it for 25 years and you can only do so much wear to the body. It changes a man. It has changed me. I can see it. I can feel it.

MONEY CALLS

Ali remained in retirement for two full years. During that time, he settled down in his homes in Chicago and Los Angeles and seemed to be content conducting business deals and living with Veronica Porche, who had become his third wife, and their two children. His career earnings totaled an estimated $50 million, but little was invested for high yield. In 1980, his need for money compelled him into the ring once again. As far as money was concerned there were about one hundred fifty people in his orbit that he did not want to let down. Some family and close friends say because of his big heart he allowed himself to get ripped off time after time. They say the softy usually turned a blind eye to extravagant spending, as well as double-dealing within his large traveling entourage. The giving did not stop there. Because of his belief that wealth should be shared with those in need complete strangers often benefited from his millions.

Without a real desire to fight again he came out of retirement to face the latest heavyweight champ. His opponent was Larry Holmes, one of the sparring partners whom he had brought to Africa when he had taken the title from Foreman.

Former Heavyweight Champion Larry Holmes

Larry Holmes became the longest reigning world heavyweight champion, lasting from 1978 to 1985. His professional record consists of 69 wins, with 44 resulting knockouts and 6 losses. Holmes, still in his prime, knew that Ali did not have a chance against him, as told Stephen Brunt for the *Facing Ali* book. He knew Ali too well. Having been a sparring partner and an Ali insider four straight years, he could anticipate the man's moves inside and outside the ring. Hurting his friend during the match is what really worried him.

"I knew one thing. He would take a punch. And I knew another thing. He would take a beating. You see, my thing is, I tried to get rid of him, but after four or five rounds I stopped. I just wanted the referee to stop it. What happens to a fighter after four or five good rounds of bang, bang, bang is they get hurt if they take those punches. You take punishment, something's got to give man." Although he won, Holmes felt bad because he beat a man too old for the game, a man he admired.

Ali was 38 years old and overweight at the time of the Holmes fight, which proved to be an embarrassment for him. The match was held in the 100-degree heat of Las Vegas and lasted eleven rounds before Herbert Muhammad stopped it. Ali threw only a couple of punches during the whole fight; these punches seemed to be so weak that they would not have hurt a child. Holmes, who respected Ali, treated the champion as gently as he could. Still, by the end of the fight, Ali had suffered a bloody nose, a cut under his right eye, and reddening under his left eye.

Ali claimed that his sluggish performance had resulted from a drug, Thyrolar, which he had been taking for a thyroid condition. He had lately been displaying alarming physical abnormalities. His speech had become noticeably slurred, and he seemed to drag his feet slightly when he walked. Still, the former champion laughed off questions about his general physical condition and stated that he was feeling fine.

RETIREMENT AT LAST

Ali certainly appeared to be doing well financially. He owned valuable real estate; he dressed well and traveled often. The one public blot in his business affairs was his association with an organization that carried his name but with which he was not involved in any other way. In 1981, Harold Smith, the president and chairman of Muhammad Ali Professional Sports, Inc., found himself at the center of a scandal that involved the embezzlement of $21.3 million from a Los Angeles branch of the Wells Fargo Bank. Smith, who went into hiding for a number of months after being sought for questioning, claimed that he was innocent of embezzlement charges and stated that he had bought the use of Ali's name for one million dollars. Ali, who said that Smith had only paid him $200,000, broke his ties with the organization after the scandal erupted.

In 1981, Ali made his last attempt at a boxing comeback— only to discover that none of the major boxers wanted to fight him. Even if they had, none of the boxing commissions in any state would have given him a license to box due to his less than perfect health. Yet Ali eventually managed to get a permit to box in the Bahamas. On December 11, 1981, he fought and lost a ten-round match against Trevor Berbick. Ali, who weighed in for the fight at 237 pounds, performed better than he had against Holmes. He even managed to stagger Berbick in the fifth round. Berbick won easily on the judges' decision.

Ali has left a lasting legacy to America: the strong, positive image of black America that he has always insisted on presenting to the world. Sportswriter Steve Cady explained the importance of this legacy in the *Times* by saying:

> Like so many other black people I love Ali because he is intolerable to America. His significance to me is a thousandfold. For a black man to exist he must be the greatest. He must say it over and over again, because white people might forget.

Muhammad Ali will not let anyone forget who he is and where he came from. Ali should not have fought against Holmes and Berbick. Those matches certainly offered another payday, and, perhaps, Ali stepped in the ring to prove to himself that he was still vital and young. Actually, he was neither—as would be attested to three years later. In September 1984, he was hospitalized for diagnostic tests to determine the cause of his worsening speech slur, listlessness, and difficulty in movement. Doctors at Columbia-Presbyterian Hospital in New York City discovered that Ali was suffering from Parkinson's syndrome, which manifests symptoms of Parkinson's disease. Ali's illness had been brought about by blows that had been delivered during his boxing career.

If left untreated, Parkinson's disease usually becomes a degenerative disease; its effects will become worse over time, until its victim is severely handicapped. Even though

Ali began showing signs of physical deterioration in the early 1980s and his last professional fight took place in 1981 against Trevor Berbick. In 1984, Ali was diagnosed with Parkinson's syndrome, said to be a direct result of the blows to his head received in the ring.

Parkinson's disease cannot be cured, its symptoms—stooped posture, slurred speech, tremor of the hands, a short-stepped gait, and slowness of movement—can be successfully treated with a group of drugs called L-dopa. This is the medication that was prescribed for Ali by the doctors at Columbia-Presbyterian Hospital.

Ali's hospitalization and the death of several fighters resulting from blows they suffered in the ring touched off a furor among physicians and the general public about boxing's role in society. Two prestigious medical publications, the *Journal of the American Medical Association* and the British journal *Lancet*, have recently released studies documenting the dangers of a career in boxing. The American Medical Association article reported on a study of 38 former boxers: More than half had suffered damage or loss of brain tissue. Tissue loss is especially dangerous because it can lead to the state of physical and mental impairment known as punch-drunk syndrome (called *dementia pugilistica* by doctors). The symptoms of punch-drunk syndrome are memory loss, eye and ear problems, slurred speech, an abnormal gait, and tremors. *Lancet* summed up its findings by stating that "the most predictable and permanent reward of a career in boxing is chronic brain damage." These two studies have added more fuel to a movement to ban boxing.

Dr. Charles Williams

There is much debate about the state of Ali's health under the care of Dr. Charles Williams, during his later years in the ring. Dr. Williams told *Muhammad Ali: His Life and Times* author Thomas Hauser that, as a physician he oversaw the health of Black Muslim leader Elijah Muhammad, the father of Ali's manager, and was contacted by that manager to handle Ali's health. Dr. Williams has this to say about prepping Ali for the Holmes fight:

"But Herbert [Muhammad] didn't call me until two weeks before the fight, so it forced me to correct things in too short a period of time. It was just too much. Ali's metabolism had to be increased to normal, plus he was getting older; too old, really. My job, as I interpreted it, was to do the best I could. The contracts were signed, Ali fights the fight: he conforms to the stipulations of the contract; and he gets paid. I didn't worry about whether he was going to win. It was stupid to think he was going to win. I just wanted to get him in good enough shape, and sure enough, he looked good." Williams successfully prepared Ali for visual inspection at the prefight weigh in.

Even though Ali is now suffering from the effects of his boxing career, he does not believe boxing should be banned. He reasons that in a society in which blacks and other minorities are given too few opportunities for advancement, boxing offers a way out of poverty. He has said, "Too many blacks are doing well in boxing, so whites want it banned. But how do I live here [gesturing to his house and antiques] without boxing. There's more deaths in football than boxing, but nobody wants to ban football. You see car races. Cars hit the wall, burn up.... Don't ban that, do they?" Although Ali still defends boxing, his days as a boxer are over.

10

Reintroduction to the World

Not all the doctors agreed on the cause of and prognosis for Ali's illness. At least one physician thought that removing his blood and cleansing it periodically would cure his problem. Muhammad's wife, Lonnie, a hometown friend whom he married in Louisville without a lot of fanfare in 1986, hoped blood detoxification would be the answer to her husband's problems. A primary physician nevertheless concurred with the popular belief that brain damage was causing the Parkinson's symptoms. According to that doctor's opinion at the time, the syndrome would not get progressively worse. (For additional information on the symptoms and treatment of this disease, enter "Parkinson's" into any search engine and browse the sites listed.)

In the midst of all of this, Ali could feel Parkinson's gripping his body, but he understood that his mind was working just fine. He knew that he had plenty of living yet to do. More than ever before, he realized that a higher meaning existed in his religion, a meaning that should set the direction of his life. The doctrines of Islam truly took hold of his thinking. By 1983, gone were the young and foolish days when he tried to fit the religion to what he wanted to do—chasing women and such. The field of boxing had introduced him to the world; Islam now gave him a bigger mission. Ali would spread a message of peace and help as many impoverished communities as possible.

Everyone around him agrees on one thing: He loves people, regardless of race, nationality, religion, or culture, and he wants people to love him back. In the past, his love of mankind frequently propelled him out the car to hand a homeless person money for shelter and a few meals. He gave to those individual strangers before it was fashionable. Just hearing about a small institution in financial straits could ignite his generosity and lead to a $100,000-donation with few questions asked.

Lonnie, Ali's fourth wife, says, "Muhammad belongs to the world." It certainly showed the night he departed a heavy-weight champion tribute dinner at which each former boxing great received a diamond-clustered championship ring. When leaving this event, Ali noticed a little girl in a wheelchair. The girl and her mother recognized him and asked if he would pose in a picture with the youngster. He did, with a smile, a hug, and a kiss on the cheek. Then he placed his championship ring in the child's hand and proceeded away. That was vintage Ali, giving what he could without expecting anything in return. This was the man who, whenever the mood struck, furnished thousands of dollars to individuals he knew, often family members, and paid the taxes on those gifts.

Of course, some individuals took advantage of him. Before he married Lonnie, he lost hundreds of thousands, even millions, of dollars in ill-advised deals such as movies, antipoverty programs and merchandising gone bad. Some funds were just scammed from this gentle man who avoids confrontation in his personal life and is unable to say no. He was like a kid in a candy store, sharing his sweet life with the people he encountered. His focus eventually changed from random gifts to fighting worldwide ills.

MAN WITH A MISSION

"People say I had a full life, but I ain't dead yet. I'm just getting started," he told author Thomas Hauser. "Fighting injustice, fighting racism, fighting crime, fighting illiteracy, fighting poverty, using this face the world knows so well, and going out and fighting for truth and different causes." Ali plunged in using his fame to open wallets and minds, to open hearts and bring people together in a style all his own. Very few challenges were considered too great, and people responded to him, with a few notable exceptions. One exception occurred on an early mission of mercy in Beirut, Lebanon.

In 1985, Lebanon was the site of Ali's unsuccessful attempt to negotiate the release of four Americans and one Saudi diplomat from Muslim extremists. Although his stated goal

DID YOU KNOW?

In November 1990, Muhammad Ali flew to Baghdad, Iraq, to negotiate with Saddam Hussein for the release of American hostages. He returned home 10 days later after liberating 15 of the 300 prisoners. Harry Brill-Edwards, one of those freed, said that he had not believed their release was imminent because they had been taunted with freedom many times before. This time freedom was true. "I suppose what impressed me most about Ali was the way he cared for everybody. He had a kind word or gesture for absolutely every person he saw," Brill-Edwards told Thomas Hauser for the Muhammad Ali biography.

The U.S. State Department provided the liberated Americans with a direct charter flight home. Ali was not invited on the charter. Brill-Edwards explained, "In the end, six of us stayed on the flight with Ali. We did it out of sheer gratitude and respect for the man, and it's the best decision I've made in a long time."

eluded him, he learned from the experience and would have more success freeing hostages from Saddam Hussein's grip in Iraq. On that occasion in 1990, he helped 15 Americans return to the United States, leaving some to think of him as their angel.

He used birthday bashes to raise funds for college scholarships and hit the solicitation trail for at-risk youth and underequipped Cuban hospitals, along with other causes, in the early 1990s. Celebrities and the man on the street gravitated to both his quiet charm and the champion mystique and provided generous donations.

Demand for the boxing icon faded for a period of time in the wake of phenomenons such as Michael Jordan and as widespread concerns about Ali's physical health stymied his moneymaking abilities. Lonnie Ali also thought it was a good time to slow down for a while. She was happy that they could spend more time on their farm in Michigan and enjoy being a loving married couple. Now that Ali's expensive boxing entourage had moved on to other opportunities, Lonnie and her husband truly could afford retirement.

She had already disentangled him from most of the crazy deals and schemes concocted by some members in his old entourage. These days, she quickly puts a stop to any misuse of his name or image through the courts if need be. Under her watch, any questionable business overtures are turned away. Lonnie, a master of business administration (MBA) graduate and an experienced businesswoman, managed the remaining $3.5 million estate in a positive direction. Ali could relax for a change.

They were living comfortably in their Michigan retreat when the situation changed drastically. The catalyst was Ali's appearance at the 1996 Olympics, where he demonstrated how capable the most recognized figure in the world could be.

Standing in front of a crowd of more than 80,000 people during the opening ceremony, Ali, although visibly spastic,

Muhammad Ali has spent his post-boxing years using his fame and wealth to fight against injustice, poverty, and many other problems around the world. He was recognized for his athletic and humanitarian greatness in 1996, when he was chosen to represent America by lighting the torch at the summer Olympic games in Atlanta.

stretched out to light the torch that would burn for the duration of the Olympics Games. Ali, for whom speech had become a challenge, needed only to smile to express his overwhelming emotions. This road to the Olympics had not been easy.

Committee members spoke with photojournalist and best friend Howard Bingham prior to the 1996 games, but they listened skeptically. It took months of discussions with both NBC and Olympic officials to convince them that Ali was up to the task. That done, officials asked everyone to keep their agreement secret. Ali was not informed until three weeks before the event, thereby ensuring that the man who loves to talk could not accidentally break the confidence.

Ali's lightness, to the thrill of event-goers, spread well beyond the Olympic torch. His presence was felt in numerous corners of the 1996 games. He attended many events around Atlanta and took time to visit the athletes in the Olympic village. As he socialized, he was determined to satisfy everyone who wished to have a picture taken with him. The International Olympic Committee (IOC) recognized Ali's continuing generosity throughout the Olympics and throughout his life by rewarding him with a gold medal to replace the 1960 gold medal that he had "lost" years before.

Muhammad Ali became much more than a spokesman for America; he became the spirit that fires up athletes and the spirit that is the Olympics. His brand of genuine charisma grew in demand. Calls came from profit-oriented corporations and nonprofit charities and government agencies. The tornado of activity swirling around this heightened success appeared daunting to Lonnie. Bookings, mail, and travel, all of which Ali loved, came in constantly. Ali was happy to respond to it all.

A DIFFERENT TYPE OF COMEBACK

In the background, Lonnie worried about her husband overdoing it and began more judicious management, but he could be stubborn when it came to certain issues, his mail being one. Despite increasing fan mail—about 35 to 68 boxes a week—Ali, ever the people person, insisted on reading each one and signing 2,000 autographs.

He would wake to morning prayer at his farm in Michigan, then tackle the letters at the worktable in his den. He would break throughout the day for meals and a couple of healthy outings. First came a walk over pristine farm acreage and later came his people time, trips to a neighboring school, church, shelter, or another type of social institution. He also studied the Qur'an daily and still found some family and friend time. There would be four more prayers between reading stacks of letters.

Ali's days at home flowed, as full and easygoing as the man himself. Generally, he was happy to conform to the wishes of family and guests—going places or doing things at home that interested them. In turn, he got his kicks sprinkling them with jokes and maybe a prank or two.

Debating the workload surrounding tons of mail was useless. Lonnie and others could advise Ali, but when his mind was made up, nothing would budge it. He most certainly would not let Parkinson's stand in his way.

He takes his affliction philosophically. "I think that too many people put me on a pedestal before and made me into an idol. And that's against Islam there are no idols in Islam. So maybe this problem I have is God's way of reminding me and every-body else what's important," he explained to Thomas Hauser.

IN HIS OWN WORDS...

Ali told Thomas Hauser for his biography:

Talking about boxing bores me now. Boxing was just to introduce me to the world. People today, they want me to talk like I used to. 'I'm the greatest! I'm the prettiest! I'm this, and I'm that!' But I don't want to do that no more. There's bigger work I got to do. The whole world is in trouble.

Lonnie arranged his schedule so that about half of their time was spent supporting charities and the other half went to companies, as wide-ranging as VitaPro and Adidas to Gillette and IBM, which paid for the privilege to use Ali's name with their products.

In 1996, the elder statesman added a campaign against hate and bigotry to his agenda after collaborating on two books with Thomas Hauser—*Healing: A Journal of Tolerance and Understanding* and *Muhammad Ali in Perspective*. He toured the world promoting humanity and peace between one person with another. By that stage, Ali's speech may have been significantly impaired from Parkinson's, but his mind worked just fine and he found a way to share his thoughts with the world through writing. In addition to the messages of tolerance from his books, 3,400 journals were distributed to high school students seen on the tour. The teenagers were encouraged to write down their reflections on brotherhood and racial awareness. According to the *Christian Science Monitor*, Ali told students, "Hating people because of their color is wrong. And it doesn't matter which color does the hating. It's plain wrong."

He continued traveling with enthusiasm and exploring the many opportunities sliding his direction. His own plight with Parkinson's could not be ignored during charitable endeavors. With Lonnie by his side, he leaped into advocacy for research to cure Parkinson's. Debuting this effort on *The Today Show* together, Lonnie announced the first study of minorities suffering from the illness. Ali since has raised thousands of dollars for Parkinson's research, in addition to enlightening Congress on the subject. The medical community holds out hope that answers lie within drug research and maybe stem cell therapies. Stem cells are microscopic units in the body. Those building blocks, which have not yet developed specialized functions, can transform into tissue for any function the body needs.

THE POWER
POSSIBLE IS
IM OSSIB
A M

Despite suffering from severe speech and motor impairment due to Parkinson's syndrome, Ali continues to spend his time working with charities and endorsing various companies. Here in 2004, Ali joins his daughter Laila, a super middleweight boxing champion, at the unveiling of an Adidas wallscape in Harlem.

ALI AND WORLD PEACE

Ali proved to be a tireless worker, making more than 130 trips for various projects in 1996. The United Nations (U.N.) decided to tap into his vigor. When the organization dispatched U.N. Messengers of Peace in 1998, Ali was counted among them. U.N. Secretary General Kofi Annan remembered him from an appearance at the organization's New York head-quarters 20 years before, when Ali delivered a message of "peace and spirituality" to the U.N. Special Committee against Apartheid in 1978. The United Nations is an international coalition dedicated to guiding and helping develop peaceful policies and economies worldwide. As one of its Messengers, Ali promotes tolerance and respect for human rights, disarmament, and drug control and provides development assistance to poor nations and to refugees and children. Ali's peaceful mission on behalf of the U.N. often takes him to remote places in Africa and Asia; the needs there are pervasive.

In 2002, he visited a new girls' school in postwar Afghanistan, where the desire for education was so strong that classes spilled into tents. Females of all ages had been banned from formal education under the Taliban government. The U.S. military, backed by an international coalition of troops, had fought a war to oust Afghanistan's Taliban leaders after

Muhammad Ali on 9/11

Muhammad Ali's press statement regarding the perpetrators of the terrorist attacks was released by a representative. It appears here, as published in the Louisville, Kentucky *Courier-Journal*.

I am a Muslim. I am an American. As an American Muslim, I want to express my deep sadness and anguish at the tremendous loss of life that occurred on Tuesday.

Islam is a religion of peace. Islam does not promote terrorism or the killing of people.

I cannot sit by and let the world think that Islam is a killing religion. It hurts me to see what radical people are doing in the name of Islam. These radicals are doing things that God is against. Muslims do not believe in violence.

If the culprits are Muslim, they have twisted the teachings of Islam. Whoever performed, or is behind, the terrorist attacks in the United States of America does not represent Islam. God is not behind assassins. Anyone involved in this must pay for their evil.

I pray that God blesses the people and families of those who were killed, and our great country.

After retiring as the greatest boxer ever, Muhammad Ali, here in 1999, began a more important career as a humanitarian. Ali's legacy is not only an inspiration to athletes but to all those with determination and spirit who want to make their mark on the world.

they refused to surrender al-Qaida terrorists. Osama bin Laden and his al-Qaida network were deemed responsible for planning and executing the attacks on the World Trade Center and the Pentagon and the aborted flight downed in Western Pennsylvania on September 11, 2001.

While in Afghanistan, Ali toured food enterprises—bakeries and such—sprouting from U.N. recovery programs. He flew to that country to shine a light on the resources needed for its reconstruction.

He also swung into motion right after that horrendous day in America, joining the two-hour celebrity telethon to raise money for 9/11 victims and their families. He was saddened by the destruction and stated that such terrorism does not represent Islam and its perpetrators should be brought to justice. He reiterated that peace is at the core of the Islamic religion and the lives of its Muslim followers.

Ali has been less definite about the continuation of the U.S. war on terrorism carried out in Iraq. Lonnie Ali has stated that her husband opposes conflict and is praying for peace there because war may not be the answer. They worry about U.S. soldiers and all civilians who have been killed or injured and hope that the U.S. will not be drawn into a quagmire during the occupation.

The hurtful things being said about Muslims as a result of these conflicts are equally troubling to the Ali family. Americans and Arabs, Muslims and Christians have much in common, which should be made known. The Muhammad Ali Center in Louisville, Kentucky is designed to expose those common-alities by heralding the values central to Ali's life. The center is scheduled to open in 2005, in large part because of Ali's fundraising abilities.

These days, Ali stands for much more than he did as a champion boxer. He is an emblem of the world's humanitari-anism. Being instrumental in more than 230 million meals reaching the hungry is only part of his recent undertakings. His crusades have shined the light of understanding on the man in the street, people suffering from famine and war, as well as a others in need across the four corners of the globe. He doesn't dismiss his incredible boxing feats, but Ali feels that his present mission and his family are his greatest achievements.

1942 *January 18* Born Cassius Clay, Jr., in Louisville, Kentucky

1954 Takes his first boxing lesson

1955 Appears in the Kentucky State Golden Gloves tournament

1959 Wins national Golden Gloves tournament

1960 Wins Golden Gloves, Amateur Athletic Union championship, and Olympic gold medal as a light heavyweight; signs with the Louisville Millionaires

1964 Beats Sonny Liston in six rounds for the heavyweight championship; announces his conversion to Islam and changes his name to Muhammad Ali

1967 Refuses induction into the armed forces; is convicted for draft evasion; his boxing license is revoked and is stripped of heavyweight title

1970 Beats Jerry Quarry in three rounds

1971 Loses to Joe Frazier in fifteen rounds for first professional loss; conviction on draft evasion charge is reversed; a law requiring diversity on Selective Service boards is enacted

1974 Beats Frazier in twelve rounds; beats George Foreman in eight rounds and wins heavyweight title

1975 Beats Frazier in fourteen rounds

1978 Loses heavyweight title to Leon Spinks in fifteen rounds; beats Spinks in fifteen rounds to regain heavyweight title for third time; addresses U.N. Special Committee against Apartheid

1980 Loses to Larry Holmes in eleven rounds

1981 Loses to Trevor Berbick in ten rounds; retires from boxing

1984 Is diagnosed as suffering from Parkinson's disease

1990 Is inducted into the International Boxing Hall of Fame

1996 Ignites the 1996 Olympic torch that burned for the duration of the games in Atlanta; received honorary gold medal

1998 Is named United Nations Messenger of Peace; unveils plans to build The Muhammad Ali Center in his hometown of Louisville, Kentucky

1999 Selected as *USA Today*'s Athlete of the Century

2001 Ignites the Olympic torch to begin its 13,500-mile trip to the Salt Lake games

2003 Wins Bambi, a prestigious German award, for his lifetime of achievement; receives Afghanistan World Foundation Freedom Award

2005 Scheduled opening of The Muhammad Ali Center

Ali, Muhammad. *The Greatest: My Own Story*. New York: Random House, 1975.

Brunt, Stephen. *Facing Ali: 15 Fighters, 15 Stories*. Toronto, Canada: Knopf, Random House Canada, 2002.

Hauser, Thomas. *Muhammad Ali His Land and Times*. New York: Touchstone, Simon and Schuster, 1991.

Mailer, Norman. *The Fight*. Boston: Little, Brown, 1975.

Schulberg, Bud. *Loser and Still Champion: Muhammad Ali*. New York: Doubleday, 1972.

Sheed, Wilfrid. *Muhammad Ali*. New York: Crowell, 1975.

Torres, Jose. *Sting Like a Bee: The Muhammad Ali Story*. New York: Abelard-Schuman, 1975.

Williams, Juan. *Eyes on the Prize: America's Civil Rights, Years 1954–1965*. New York: Penguin Books, 1988.

WEBSITES
The BBC Muhammad Ali sports coverage
http://news.bbc.co.uk/sport1/hi/boxing/specials/ali_at_60/default.stm

The *Courier-Journal* Louisville, Kentucky, newspaper
www.courier-journal.com/ali/

International Boxing Hall of Fame
www.ibhof.com

The Muhammad Ali Center
www.alicenter.org

Muhammad Ali Official Website
www.ali.com

page:

2: Associated Press, AP	55: Associated Press, AP
9: Library of Congress, LC-USZC4-3859	56: © Bettmann/CORBIS
	61: © Bettmann/CORBIS
14: Associated Press, AP	65: Associated Press, AP
17: © Bettmann/CORBIS	74: © Bettmann/CORBIS
21: Associated Press, AP	80: © Lynn Goldsmith/CORBIS
26: © Bettmann/CORBIS	83: Associated Press, AP
32: Associated Press, AP	86: Associated Press, AP
35: © Bettmann/CORBIS	91: © Bettmann/CORBIS
36: Associated Press, AP	97: © William Coupon/CORBIS
42: Associated Press, AP	104: Associated Press, AP/Doug Mills
45: Associated Press, AP	108: Associated Press, AP/Ed Bailey
49: Associated Press, AP	110: © Michael Brennan/CORBIS
53: Associated Press, AP	

Cover: Associated Press, AP/Richard Drew

ABOUT THE AUTHOR

Jack Rummel is a freelancer writer who lives in Hoboken, New Jersey. He is also the author of *Malcolm X* and *Langston Hughes* in the BLACK AMERICANS OF ACHIEVEMENT series.

AUTHOR OF ADDITIONAL TEXT, LEGACY EDITION

Gloria Blakely is a graduate of the Howard University honors program and is an active member of the Philadelphia Association of Black Journalists in Philadelphia, PA where she resides. She also has been listed among up and coming children's book writers in *Something About the Authors* by Gales Services and was bestowed two writing awards by the 2003 Philadelphia Writers' Conference. She is also the author of *Jesse Jackson* and *Rosa Parks* in the BLACK AMERICANS OF ACHIEVEMENT series.

CONSULTING EDITOR, REVISED EDITION

Heather Lehr Wagner is a writer and editor. She is the author of 30 books exploring social and political issues and focusing on the lives of prominent Americans and has contributed to biographies of Harriet Tubman, Sojourner Truth, Thurgood Marshall, Malcolm X, Frederick Douglass, and Martin Luther King, Jr., in the BLACK AMERICANS OF ACHIEVEMENT legacy series. She earned a BA in political science from Duke University and an MA in government from the College of William and Mary. She lives with her husband and family in Pennsylvania.

CONSULTING EDITOR, FIRST EDITION

Nathan Irvin Huggins was W.E.B. Du Bois Professor of History and Director of the W.E.B. Du Bois Institute for Afro-American Research at Harvard University. He previously taught at Columbia University. Professor Huggins was the author of numerous books, including *Black Odyssey: The Afro-American Ordeal in Slavery*, *The Harlem Renaissance*, and *Slave and Citizen: The Life of Frederick Douglass*. Nathan I. Huggins died in 1989.